FIBRES to FABRICS

FIBRES to FABRICS

Techniques and Projects for Handspinners

Hazel Clark

B. T. Batsford, London

ISBN 0 7134 46161

Typeset by Keyspools Ltd, Golborne Lancs,
and printed in Great Britain by
Anchor Brendon Ltd
Tiptree, Essex

for the publishers
B. T. Batsford Ltd.
4 Fitzhardinge Street London W1H 0AH

Contents

Acknowledgement

I would like to thank Quantum Photography of
Leeds, who took all the pictures; my 'class of 83'
at Baildon; Haldane & Co. of Gateside, Cupar,
Fife, equipment suppliers; Pat and Annie
McEvoy; Hodder & Stoughton, for permission to
use a pattern from Star Crochet; and my
husband Brian, who polished my original
manuscript and typed it.

This book is dedicated to my late father, Prof. G.
N. Patchett, whose example I have been proud
to follow.

Preface

The craft of handspinning may not be as domestically or commercially essential as it once was, but despite all the advances of modern technology it is currently enjoying a revival – in common with many other traditional occupations.

Whatever the reasons for this resurgence of interest, we have not yet reached the stage where people are queuing at the handspinner's door eager to buy handspun yarns. Nowadays in Britain, although we spin for pleasure it is almost certainly as a means to an end: the fruits of the handspinner's labours offer the exciting prospect of creating something uniquely appealing.

For the beginner or the experienced handspinner, there are many books, some of them excellent and very comprehensive. But most of them concentrate on 'how to do it' without offering detailed suggestions, ideas and inspiration on how to make the best use of all that handspun yarn once you have mastered the craft.

That is why this project book has been written.

Not all the projects will appeal to everyone, but I hope they will spark off ideas – in which case the basic methods and techniques can easily be adapted to suit personal tastes. I have assumed that the reader will have a basic knowledge of spinning already, although anyone new to spinning should have little difficulty in tackling several of the projects. If this book inspires anyone to take up handspinning for the first time, you may be encouraged to know that a good number of the projects were undertaken by my students in their first year.

The more experienced handspinners will also, I think, find plenty of scope along with a number of new ideas, some useful tips and hints, and several methods and techniques which have not, so far as I know, been published elsewhere.

Materials and Basic Techniques

Introduction

This is not intended to be a textbook on handspinning, but some introductory notes are necessary to clarify some of the terms used and methods described in the following projects. Some of the more unusual techniques like feltmaking, Navajo plying and grafting are fully detailed as they occur in a particular project.

SPINNING WHEELS

Although I have accumulated a collection of spinning wheels and accessories, I realise that most spinners have one wheel with perhaps a large flyer unit. None of the projects requires you to rush out and buy another wheel; in fact, many of them can be accomplished with a simple drop spindle. So my choice of wheel and ratio for each project should be taken only as a guide. As a matter of interest, the wheels I used for the projects described in this book were: an Ashford bobbin driven Indian wheel, an antique Scandinavian wheel with a large supply of whorls, a double band reproduction upright Shetland wheel, and an Ashford traditional wheel with a jumbo flyer attachment.

Whatever wheel you use, it should have two different wheel-to-pulley ratios if possible. For extra-bulky yarns, you will need a large flyer. Good spinning wheels run smoothly, treadle effortlessly and have reasonably sized bobbins.

Some spinners prefer double band wheels, others single band. Wheels are now available which incorporate both drive systems. Most beginners find it easier to use the single band wheel with a Scotch tension, because the adjustment for the drive band and bobbin take-up are controlled by separate knobs.

A drop spindle is a useful, inexpensive tool by which to learn spinning. A lightweight spindle is needed for fine yarns and a larger, heavy spindle for thick yarns and for plying.

RATIOS

To obtain the right amount of twist to your yarn, the ratio of wheel to pulley is important. Here is an easy way to determine that ratio: tie a piece of thread to one of the wheel spindles and another piece to an arm of the flyer. Start with the marked spindle in the 12 o'clock position and with the marked flyer arm uppermost. Now turn the wheel slowly by hand one revolution and at the same time count the number of times the flyer revolves. If, for example, it turns seven times, the ratio is expressed as 7:1. A large diameter wheel with a small spindle pulley will give a high ratio, whereas a small cottage-style wheel with a similar-sized pulley will give a low ratio.

If your wheel has only a low ratio (6:1 and under) and you want to make a high twist yarn, then you must treadle quickly. The reverse – a high ratio wheel (say 15:1) – used to make a low twist yarn is not so simple, and in some cases it will be impossible for the hands to work fast

1. From left to right: Ashford Traditional with distaff, antique Scandinavian, Haldane's Shetland, 'Indian' bulk spinner. In the foreground are a Navajo spindle and a drop spindle

enough to draft out the long length necessary for each pump of the treadle.

Few spinners seem to measure the lengths of their hanks and weigh them accurately in order to calculate the yarn count, so I have not given specific twist per inch details and yarn counts for each project. Instead, actual size photographs of yarns are shown, together with descriptions, wheel ratios and spinning methods. A rough guide for the correct amount of twist in yarns is:

use a LOW ratio when spinning	*use a HIGH ratio when spinning*
thick yarns	fine yarns
long fibres	short fibres
straight from the fleece	warp yarns
single ply yarns	woollen long draw
a soft, bulky yarn with Navajo plying technique	yarns for hardwearing outer garments

SPINNING METHODS

The three basic spinning methods referred to in the projects are: worsted short draw (often termed simply 'short draw' in many books), woollen short draw, and woollen long draw.

Students often find worsted short draw the easiest technique to learn first. It is similar to the

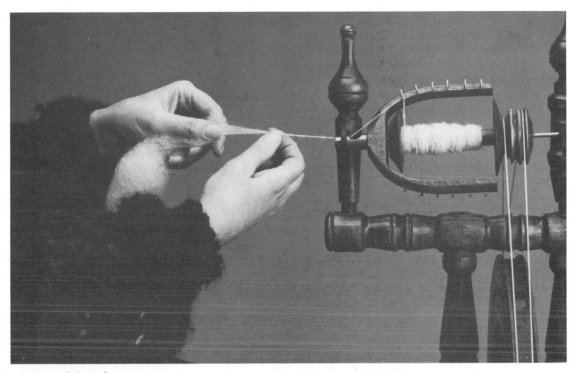

2. Worsted short draw

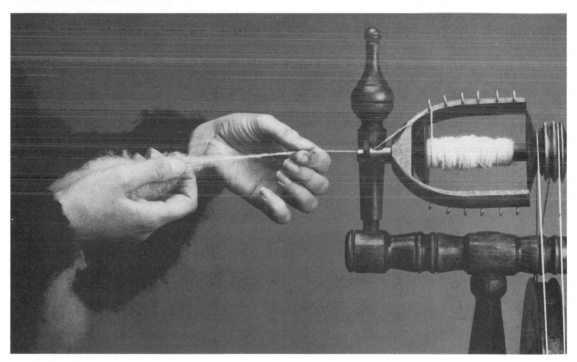

3. Woollen draw

drop spindle method. Then the woollen short draw method is learned, and finally the woollen long draw. I have given the method used in each project only as a guide.

Worsted short draw is used mostly for spinning long fibres (about 4 inches – 10 cm – and over) and produces a smooth, less 'hairy' yarn. It is also used for novelty yarns, and for fibres needing a free hand for teasing whilst the other is controlling the twist. In drafting, the fibres are pulled forward (forcing many to lie parallel) from the fibre supply before the twist is allowed to run down. In a worsted draw, the twist never enters the fibre supply. Right-handed spinners normally use the right hand to draw and control the twist, with the left hand controlling the fibre supply.

With woollen draws however, the twist does enter the fibre supply. The hand holding the fibre is pulled back and in so doing controls the thickness of the yarn. Drawing back quickly will result in a fine yarn, drawing back slowly gives the twist chance to catch up with more fibres and gives a thicker yarn. The other hand (in front) controls the amount of twist sent down the yarn and also controls tension. Woollen draw methods produce a light and airy, warm and fluffy yarn. This technique is used for shorter fibres (usually no longer than $3\frac{1}{2}$ inches – 9 cm) but to produce even yarns good fibre preparation is essential, because there is less opportunity to tease out any lumps as you go along.

With the short draw woollen method, the spinner draws back, just ahead of the twist, for a short distance (usually just over the knee) before allowing the yarn to enter the orifice. With the long draw woollen method there is an initial build-up of twist, when the spinner treadles a few times – holding the yarn some 9 inches (23 cm) from the orifice – before starting to draw back. The draw starts by putting your front hand, usually the left, on the yarn 4 to 5 inches (6.5 to 12.5 cm) from the orifice. The right hand then draws the fibres back.

When the twist runs out one third to one half of the way through this long draw, the left hand releases more twist. It continues to control the

4. Woollen long draw

amount of twist let through until the right hand is drawn fully back. The yarn is then let immediately into the orifice – unless of course it has insufficient twist. In this case the spinner will treadle a couple of times before letting the yarn in. This initial build-up of twist plus the long draw makes this a fast way of spinning. It is easy to acquire a rhythm, thus ensuring that each length of yarn spun has the same amount of twist. With a medium fine yarn that has to be plied I find that three treadles (on a 10:5 ratio) for the first build-up of twist, then a further seven treadles, give me enough twist to complete the draw.

LOOMS

Many spinners are discouraged from using their handspun for weaving because of the high cost of the necessary equipment or the space it might occupy. Most of my projects involve using simple looms. In fact, two of the looms can easily be made at home. By strengthening the Navajo loom, projects such as the tapestry can be woven without needing a floor loom.

One of the cheapest and smallest looms is the rigid heddle, and this I have used for two of the projects, including a full-size jacket woven on an 18 inch loom. The success of all the woven items described depends on the colour and texture of your handspun yarns and the way you control them, rather than on structural weaves – which need multi-shaft looms.

CHOICE OF FLEECE

Local farmers are the main source of my fleeces, and the ones mentioned are easily obtained near to my workshop in Yorkshire. A good alternative is the British Wool Marketing Board, Oak Mills, Clayton, Bradford, who will send a price list on request and then mail fleeces to you.

Jacob wool is understandably popular with handspinners because of its beautiful natural colours. But beware – Jacob varies in quality more than any other British breed I have encountered, possibly because it's kept in small flocks in widely differing conditions and a lot of interbreeding has taken place. A Jacob fleece may be hairy and coarse with a $6\frac{1}{2}$ inch (16 cm) staple or short, fine and bouncy with a $2\frac{3}{4}$ inch (7 cm) staple. Some fleeces are kempy (lots of short, blunt shed hairs) and others not.

All fleeces vary within the breed and should be examined carefully before buying. Here are some hints:

1. Decide on the project and which fleece type you need (hill, lustre or down).
2. Open out the fleece if possible.
3. Check for colour variation. Do you want a uniform colour for a large project or are you using it for several (in which case thorough blending is not so important)?
4. Is it clean? Straw and burrs may take hours to remove.
5. Is it a very greasy fleece and has it begun to stain yellow?
6. Look at the cut side. Are there many second cuts? A few are permissible. A lot are the result of poor shearing and can be very frustrating for the spinner.
7. Is it matted (cotty)? Some may be a little matted at the belly and britch, but if matted throughout then preparation is going to be very difficult.
8. Pull a lock from the shoulder area. Check for a weak' band. Pull gently. The fibres shouldn't be brittle.
9. Check for hairs and kemp, depending on the type of fleece.
10. Are there many different qualities throughout the fleece? e.g. hairy rump, weathered back, good shoulders, short matted belly and legs. How much sorting are you prepared to do?
11. Is it a new fleece? Do the fibres slide past each other or has the grease set? Has it spent a year in the farmer's barn?
12. Look for signs of moths, if you suspect it's been lying around. Avoid it like the plague if it is contaminated. They are difficult to get rid of and will surely spread to your other fleeces. A fat grub impaled on your handcarder is not one of the joys of handspinning!

There are three main groups of breeds in Britain: hill, lustre and down. If you cannot obtain the fleece described in a particular project, choose an alternative from the same group.

Hill (coarse wool)	*Lustre* (shiny, long)	*Down* (short, fine)
Black Welsh Mountain	Teeswater Wensleydale	Clun Forest Texel
Blackface	Leicester	Devon
Cheviot	Longwool	Closewool
Dalesbred	Blueface	Dorset Horn
Herdwick	Leicester	Dorset Down
Lonk	Dartmoor	Hampshire
Rough Fell	Lincoln	Down
Swaledale	Longwool	Jacob
Welsh Mountain	Devon	Kerry Hill
	Longwool	Llanwenog
	(the last three	Oxford Down
	are a little	Hill Radnor
	coarser)	Ryeland
	Romney	Shetland
	Masham (semi-	Suffolk
	lustre cross	Shropshire
	breed)	Southdown

This list is by no means comprehensive. If you still have difficulty choosing the right fleece consult *British Sheep Breeds – Their Wool and its Uses*, obtainable from the British Wool Marketing Board.

For further information on specific aspects and on general methods and techniques relating to the projects I describe, I have listed a number of books in the bibliography which I, and others, have found particularly useful and worthy of a place in the handspinners library.

Throughout the book, the metric and imperial sizes and quantities given are not necessarily the exact equivalent of each other.

KEY TO ABBREVIATIONS USED IN PATTERNS

Crochet

ch	chain
dc	double crochet (USA – single crochet)
htr	half treble (USA – half double crochet)
tr	treble (USA double crochet)
dtr	double treble (USA – treble)
tr tr	triple treble (USA – double treble)
quad tr	quadruple treble (USA triple treble)
s s	slip stitch
st (s)	stitch(es)

inc	increase
dec	decrease
sp	space

Knitting

alt	alternately
beg	beginning
cont	continue
dec	decrease, decreasing
fol	following
gst	garter stitch
inc	increase, increasing
K	knit
P	purl
psso	pass slipped stitch over
rem	remain(ing)
rep	repeat
rs	right side
sl	slip
st(s)	stitch(es)
st st	stocking stitch
tog	together
ws	wrong side
yf	yarn forward
yo	yarn over
yrn	yarn round needle
tbl	through back of loop
M1	make one

1 Thick pile floor rug

Meg joined my spinning class on doctor's advice. She had injured her hand in a car accident and handspinning was prescribed as an ideal way of exercising the damaged muscles. She soon became proficient at spinning a thick and even yarn. But, never having learned to knit or crochet, Meg was at a loss to know what to do with her ever-increasing stock of handspun yarn. What skill could she acquire quickly which would result in a useful article? The idea of making a rug with a latch hook was greeted with enthusiasm. Here was something needing little skill (even small children can get involved), a simple tool, and which can be worked on whilst watching TV or chatting to friends.

I decided to start my own rug and take it along to class as an example. I had been saving the coarser parts of many fleeces for just such a project. My local market sells rug canvas offcuts so I bought a piece just over 5 feet (1.5 metres) long – rather bigger than I wanted but an irresistable bargain at £1. It had three squares to the inch (2.5 cm).

Many intricate and beautiful geometric patterns can be made on a rug canvas, as each hole can have a different colour of pile knotted in. To make a patterned rug, count off the squares and mark the pattern on the canvas. I planned my rug to be dark brown at each end, shading gradually to a white centre. In this case there was no need to mark the canvas, and I decided to work on both

ends alternately to enable me to match the shading. All the dark wool was mixed and then weighed to give equal amounts for each end. After hooking some 6 inches (15 cm) at each end I realised what an immese task I had set myself. It is a very slow process. How I wished I had cut that bargain canvas to a smaller size, but this time it was too late – I was committed!

A floor rug wears better if the yarn used is from a long staple wool, spun worsted or semi-worsted. The cut ends will then, in time, wear to a point, having shed only a few of the cut fibres. If short staple fibres and a woollen preparation and spinning method are used, the fibres will quickly come loose from the cut yarn and continue to do so. Consequently, the rug soon wears out.

To achieve a more worsted yarn from the carders, the webs are rolled in the opposite direction to that of rolags, thereby keeping most of the fibres parallel (see fig. 7). I carded almost half the wool on handcarders before finally deciding to invest in a drum carder. I had been tempted to buy one before, but the scale of this project convinced me of its value. The drum carder certainly made the job much easier. Each wide drum web was divided lengthways into three before spinning (each with the fibres lying parallel).

The yarn was spun on a Scotch tension wheel with a jumbo flyer (large bobbins and large orifice) with a 4.3:1 ratio. A thick singles yarn,

5. Fifteen pounds (6.8 kilos) of the coarser parts of Jacob, Lonk and Texel fleeces went into the making of this 5 ft by 3 ft (152 by 91 cm) thick pile rug in natural shades

with a little overtwist, was spun using a worsted draw. This was then hanked. At this stage, you can get quite rough with the yarn, encouraging it to felt a little by placing it in very hot water, then cold, for a few times before the actual wash. The cut ends will shed less if the yarn is slightly felted.

I worked out the desired depth of pile by cutting the yarn to various lengths and making test knots on the canvas. The chosen depth of pile was $1\frac{1}{4}$ inches (3 cm) so each cut yarn, including the knot, measured $4\frac{1}{2}$ inches (11.5 cm). A guide for wrapping rug wool round can be bought at craft shops, but I made my own easily by using a piece of tongued and grooved board sawn to the right size and making use of the machined groove.

Some of my yarn was a little too thick to knot

6.

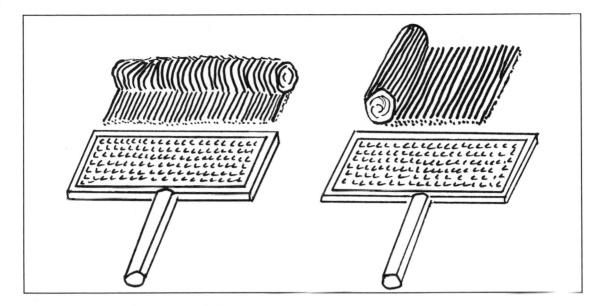

7. Web rolled for woollen spinning (left), and web rolled for worsted spinning (right)

easily through the canvas, making the work hard. In fact I could have used every other square instead of every single one and still made a thick rug, but in half the time. It would have been easier to hook the rug had I spun the same weight of wool but made the yarn slightly thinner and the pile longer. However, all my hard labour was amply rewarded: I have a very distinctive rug with a pile so dense that it's unbelievably luxurious to sit or walk on.

Some people back rugs like these with sacking or strong fabric, but I prefer to leave mine unbacked. Any dirt or grit can then work its way through the pile and be shaken out. Backing a rug traps the dirt, and any build-up of grit between rug canvas and backing produces an abrasive action and may shorten the life of the rug.

2 Shawls

Shawls always seem to be in fashion, whether worn with an evening dress or as an alternative to a cardigan, tied over a top coat or worn gipsy-style round the waist.

The shawls I describe here are quick and easy to crochet, making them ideal projects for anyone new to handspinning. I think they look most attractive when different natural shades of wool are used. I enjoy blending various shades on my handcarders and then spinning from the rolags at random. The shawl will then have patches of colour throughout, as in shawls 1 and 3 illustrated (see fig. 8). With a piebald fleece you can start the shawl in a dark colour, gradually adding more white wool to the rolags until the shawl is shaded to white. The process may then be reversed or repeated, as illustrated in shawl 2. If you use a multi-shaded handspun yarn, the design possibilites are limitless, even with such a simple shape and stitch, and each time you make one of these shawls it will by truly unique. A single-colour fleece looks good too, either spun very fine for a delicate shawl or thicker and uneven to give texture and character.

I spun a single ply yarn on a single band wheel (ratio 6.5:1), but could equally well have used a drop spindle. Jacob wool used for all three shawls was fine with an average staple length of three inches (7.5 cm), enabling me to use the long draw method of spinning. The yarn was given just enough twist to hold the fibres together. The wool was clean enough to crochet the yarn straight from the bobbin (after placing it on a lazy kate) without washing or setting the twist. I have to admit this is the only article I have ever crocheted straight from the greasy wool. I would not advise attempting it with a badly soiled fleece or if using an overtwisted yarn because dirt may remain in the very twisted areas even after washing. The crocheted shawl is dull, greasy and stiff to handle until washed, and it's hard to resist the temptation to give it a quick soak halfway through making up just to watch the colours and the wool spring to life! With no waiting for yarn to be washed and dried, it is enjoyable to be working on the shawl less than an hour after selecting the raw fleece. But you may prefer to treat your yarn more conventionally, washing it in hank form before making up.

The pattern starts at the top centre and you work the shawl outwards. The first few inches are completed surprisingly quickly – very encouraging for beginner and experienced spinner alike. When all the yarn from my first full bobbin was used, the shawl appeared to be one third finished. It does grow much more slowly however as you near the bottom edge. The pattern is as follows:

Row One 8ch, ss in first stitch to form a circle.
Row Two 3ch (counts as a tr), 1 tr, 2ch, 2tr, 2ch, 2tr, 2ch, 2tr. Turn. (Four tr groups made)

8. Three crocheted shawls from one simple, basic pattern and one Jacob fleece. Shawl no. 1 (right) weighs 4 oz (90 g), shawl no. 2 (top left) weighs 6 oz (150 g) and shawl no. 3 (bottom left) weighs 8 oz (200g)

Row Three   3ch (counts as a tr); 1tr above next to last of previous row, 2ch, 2tr in space, 2ch, in next space (middle space) work (2tr, 2ch, 2tr) 2ch, 2tr in space, 2ch, 2tr above first two tr of previous row. Turn. (Six tr groups made)

Row Four   3ch (counts as a tr), 1tr above next to last tr of previous row, 2ch, 2tr in space, 2ch, 2tr in space, 2ch, in next space (middle space) work (2tr, 2ch, 2tr), 2ch, 2tr in space, 2ch, 2tr in space, 2ch, 2tr above first two tr of previous row. Turn. (Eight tr groups made)

Continue in this way, always increasing in the middle space, and keeping the two treble border on each row at the edge.

The shawl (no. 1) was made with a fine yarn

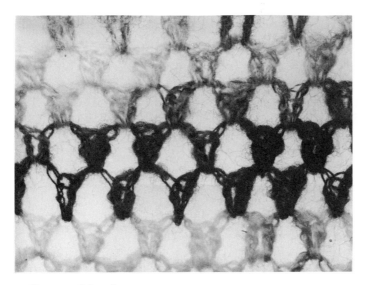

9. Close up of shawl no. 1

and hung so well I decided to emphasise its delicacy by finishing the lower edge with an appropriately fine scalloped border. Here is the pattern for shawl no. 1's edge:

In each 2ch space work 1dc, 1htr, 1tr, 1htr, 1dc to end.

No. 2 shawl was made from thicker yarn, and a thick fringe was added using yarn plied the Navajo Indian way (the technique is described on page 128. This method produces a three-ply yarn from one bobbin of singles yarn. The main advantage is in the way the colours in the plied yarn are kept separate. There is little harsh contrast of colours as when two random singles are plied normally, and because this shawl is shaded I wanted to avoid a fringe with a 'tweed' effect. If a singles yarn is used, the yarn will have

to be washed and dried under tension to prevent a kinked fringe.

When I had crocheted no. 3 shawl to the desired length, I still had quite a lot of yarn left and so decided to make a wide frill. This is a pretty and unusual alternative to a fringe.

Row One	* 2tr above 2tr of previous row, 2ch, 2tr in space, 2ch, repeat from * , 2tr above 2tr of previous row.
Row Two	Work as first row.
Row Three	In each 2ch space work: 1dc, 1htr, 2tr, 1htr, 1dc.

3 Sheep tapestry

My inspiration for this woven tapestry came from a magnificent Teeswater lustre fleece (see colour plate 1). I had already carded and spun some of the wool, but the shiny, crimped locks looked so fascinating that I wanted to find a way of using them just as they were. The result was a striking portrait of a Teeswater sheep with an authentic fleece made up by knotting in those lovely locks.

The same method can be used to portray any breed whose fleece you can obtain. Luckily, Teeswaters graze near my workshop so there were plenty of live models for me to observe. I also worked from a photograph in a British Wool Marketing Board publication.

A 33 inch upright rug loom was used, with a three dent per inch rug reed sleyed six double ends per inch. The warp was cotton.

Although the animal could have been portrayed on a neutral background, or even in a detailed pastoral setting, I chose a simple but colourful combination of hilly rough pasture and sky. Both undyed and natural or vegetable dyed yarns were used. The weft yarns for this background were all spun from Suffolk wool and, apart from some naturally black, all were dyed in the fleece.

The greens came from bracken (Pteridium aquilinum) using alum and chrome mordants. Some books advise gathering new shoots a few inches high, but these did not work well for me. The topmost fronds of maturer plants gave stronger greens. You should gather the equivalent weight of the wool to be dyed. Subtler greens and yellows came from privet (Ligustrum vulgare) and from rhubarb (Rheum rhaponticum) with alum as the mordant. For the sky, I used that traditional source of blue, woad (Isatis tinctoria). Grown easily from seed in a corner of my garden, the plant's leaves were harvested in its second year when it is some three feet tall and due to flower for the first time.

Only after my second attempt at making the dye, did I get a true sky blue. For some reason, my first effort resulted in a very pale blue. But combining the two, though I was not to know it at the time, proved to be a stroke of artistic luck. After weaving, the very pale blue faded to pink. The subtle hint of sunset in the sky was much admired!

Different shades should be sorted into piles around the loom, so they can all be seen at a glance, and you work just as a painter would with her palette. They can be mixed on carders, giving endless variations, or used straight from the pile.

To spin a fine to medium singles yarn, using a worsted draw, I keep a little Shetland wheel close by the loom. The wool is spun with just enough twist to make a workable yarn – without the twist being set. The yarn is then wound from the spinning wheel bobbin on to wooden tapestry bobbins. When these run out, I make finger

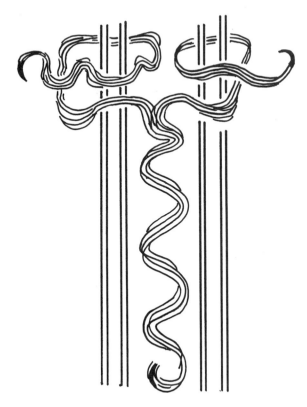

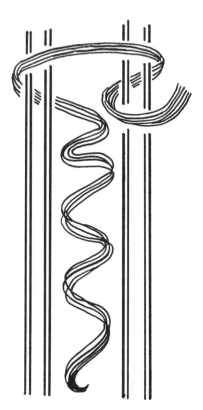

10.

11. Modified Ghiordes knot

hanks – although these are more difficult to work with when using a singles yarn without a set twist. With care, you should be able to avoid knotting when drawing. There is a great advantage in being able to blend, spin and weave without any intermediate process hampering the creative flow.

The rough pasture hilly background to the sheep portrait is woven by the curved weft technique. It is important not to pack too much weft in or the tapestry will not lie flat. For the sheep itself, the Teeswater locks were sorted: some suitable for the bulk of the body, the finer ones for the head, the most attractive crimped locks for the outline (where they show more) and finally 15 or so specially suitable locks for the fringe on the head – an endearing feature of this particular breed. Despite one careful wash, most of the fleece looked as though it needed another.

But I decided that the greyish tinge lent a touch of authenticity.

With the help of a photograph, I drew a simple cartoon of the sheep as a guide and marked a rough outline on the warp. After weaving the background, including the legs, for several inches, I began knotting in the locks. For the body I shortened the locks by about a half to match the smaller scale of my tapestry Teeswater. The discarded wool, along with other spare bits of fleece, was carded and spun into yarn for the plain weaving between the rows of knotted locks.

The first rows of knotted locks were inserted by dividing the staple at the cut end for about $1\frac{1}{2}$ inches and wrapping around two working warp ends (see fig. 10). Then the two free ends were woven into the next shed so that only the main lock hung from the surface of the tapestry. At first I wove six or seven rows of tabby between each row of locks, but as the animal grew I wanted the shape to fill out so the tabby rows became fewer. After weaving about half of the body, I changed gradually to a different method of knotting in order to give the sheep more bulk. This second knot leaves the cut ends free on the face of the weaving and so helps to pack out the locks. Known as a Ghiordes or Turkish knot, it is quicker to make than my first improvised knot. Unlike the true Turkish with ends of equal length, my version of the knot has a short end of an inch or so – just enough to make the knot firm (see fig. II).

For the sheep's face, black Suffolk was used for the lines of the nose and mouth. A well-carded mixture of black and white gave a uniform grey for the rest of the nose area. Light shading was achieved by laying in a few white fibres in an open shed on top of the grey weft. With this method, I was able to control very easily the detail of the face. The finest locks from the fleece had been set aside for the face: here the knotted samples are $\frac{1}{4}$ inch long and the wool so fine that I used a balanced Turkish knot – pointed staple at one side and the cut side fluffed out to add realism.

The blues of the sky were woven in short horizontal bands, perfectly straight, in contrast to the curved weft of the hills.

After cutting the work from the loom, both warp fringes were plaited. The top one was sewn to itself, forming a series of plaited loops to take a length of wood dowelling.

The hanging has almost become a family pet. Tessa, as she has been christened is so tactile that no-one can resist patting and stroking her!

4 Dog hair scarf

Yarn spun from dog hair is highly prized by some people, often for sentimental reasons rather than for its quality. Once I spun some hair from my own dog, a Golden Retriever, and ended up with a rather weak-fibred waistcoat. My mistake was in trying to use only 100 per cent pure family pet. The yarn would have been much stronger and more suitable for a garment had I first of all blended it with a little wool.

But there are breeds whose hair can be spun satisfactorily without blending. A friend gave me a small bag of very greyish-looking hair from her Samoyed dog. It produced an incredibly soft, light and fluffy scarf. This time I spun several sample yarns until I was convinced the fibre was strong enough to make a yarn suitable for a scarf. With the right amount of twist, the hair made a beautiful fine and strong yarn. The scarf was much admired in its own right and not merely because of its curious or sentimental origins.

Before spinning, I mixed the hair thoroughly because some fibres were a little longer than others, although most were about an inch long and quite kinky. Some I fluffed up by hand. The more compressed fibres were opened up easily with a few light strokes of the handcarders. A light spray of olive oil emulsion (20 per cent oil, 80 per cent water plus a few drops of ammonia) prevented the light fibres from flying round the room as I worked.

The hair was spun on a double band wheel using a small spindle whorl to give a ratio of 12:1. I used the woollen shortdraw method: drawing the fibres out just ahead of the twist with a draw of about 11 inches (28 cm) before letting the yarn into the wheel. I could have used the long draw method, but I found it easier to have a dark cloth on my knee and draw back over it. In this way I could see better and control such a fine yarn. I used very little draw-in tension, keeping the band on the wheel quite slack, especially at first.

The two fine singles were plied together. As most fine dog hair tends to felt easily, I washed the hanks gently, giving them a soak first and then a wash in mild detergent. Once dry, the yarn fluffed up and became beautifully white.

For such a fine and attractive yarn I chose a simple, lacy pattern which produced a delicate scalloped edge to my scarf and showed as much of the yarn as possible. After trying several needle sizes, I decided on a size 8 (4 mm).

LACE PATTERN

Row One   K3, k2 tog * . k4, yo, k1, yo, k4, k3 tog, rep from * to last 14 st then k4, yo, k1, yo, k4, k2 tog, k3.

Row Two   K.

12. Weighing only 1¼ oz (35 g) this Samoyed hair scarf measures
48 inches by 15 inches (122 cm by 38 cm)

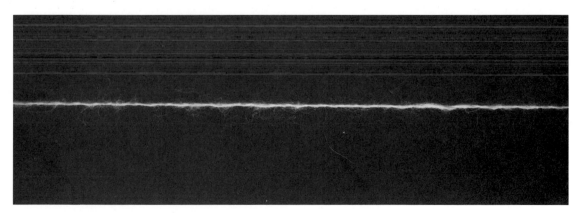

13.

5 Shetland waistcoat

Many people buying knitwear with a 'Shetland' label must be under the impression that it is wool from the Shetland breed of sheep, or wool which comes from any kind of sheep kept on the Shetland Isles. Not so! The word Shetland has become a misnomer. Nowadays it is widely used to describe a wool type or blend. It is often even applied to an imported wool blend which may, for example, come from New Zealand. The Shetland islanders are none too happy about this state of affairs.

In Britain, the genuine Shetland sheep is classified as a rare breed, but even so handspinners should have little difficulty obtaining a fleece. Commercially speaking, all the wool from one year's clip wouldn't be enough to keep my local store stocked with true Shetland jumpers. That is why I value my real Shetland fleeces. It is one of the smallest British breeds, producing on average a fleece of one to one and a half kilos. The wool may be white, grey or moorit (as the lovely ginger-brown colour is known). The white is always the finest. Average staple length is 4 inches (10 cm).

I persuaded a farmer friend to buy five purebred Shetland ewes from a Rare Breeds Survival Trust Centre. One came free because she had a 'broken mouth'. All were more than four years old, but we were assured they were a hardy, long-lived breed and would supply many more lambs and fleeces. The first fleeces from these old ladies were not spectacular. They were slightly matted, very short (about an inch) and dirty, but I was determined to make the best of each one. Two were dark grey and the rest moorit.

Part of the bargain was to spin one of the moorit fleeces for the farmer's wife to knit up. Because it was so dirty and the grease was beginning to harden, I decided to give it a wash before spinning. As the staple was so short, it lent itself to careful carding and spinning into a very fine yarn. But I knew she did not want to spend hours knitting something so fine, so I decided to experiment. The tips of each lock were honey-coloured and during carding these tips were blended in, which seemed a pity, so I decided to spin straight from the fleece, making a yarn in which the two colours – ginger-brown and honey – were distinct.

The washed fleece was laid out and sorted for colour and staple length. I ended up with three piles: one with very short fibres of about $\frac{1}{2}$ inch, one with medium length fibres and one with longer fibres, which also tended to be coarser and darker in colour (these were mainly from the rump or britch area). I mixed the wool as I went along, taking a handful from each pile before spinning. Each batch I took was still matted at the base of the fibres (a condition more common in older sheep's fleeces) and needed opening up, which I did by careful teasing, trying to free the fibres from each other at the base of the locks yet keeping the tips intact. I used my flick carder on some obstinate, matted clumps.

14.

The wool was then spun on a Scotch tension wheel with a 6.5:1 ratio. I treadled slowly and used a worsted short draw spinning method. This enabled me to guide the tips of the locks into the twist, whilst at the same time drawing back (with my left hand) the fibres at the base of the lock. At first glance it looked the kind of yarn an in-experienced spinner might produce, having thick blond slubs with a darker, thinner and smoother yarn in between. Provided I treadled slowly it was quite easy to spin, except for the very short and matted portions which were more difficult to draw out. The two singles were then plied, giving an unusual textured yarn. My friend the farmer's wife was delighted.

Having spun one fleece and given the yarn away, I decided to make the next one into a waistcoat for myself. After weighing a few of my sleeveless tops as a guide, I realised I would need

every bit of the fleece – even the short matted bits – so I prepared and spun it exactly as before. The resultant attractive, bouncy and textured yarn was knitted in plain stitch to show it off to best advantage. I chose a reverse stocking stitch, which exaggerated the rough texture. After trying various needles, I chose a size 7 (4.5 mm) which gave a compact but not hard fabric. At a glance it is hard to tell if the waistcoat is woven or knitted. I have washed and worn this garment many times, but it shows no sign of piling, as you might expect from such a textured, short-fibre yarn.

PATTERN

The pattern is for a 34/36 inch (87/91 cm) bust waistcoat (see fig. 15). Tension is 4 st to 3 cm and seven rows to 3 cm.

Cast on 134 sts with size 7 (4.5 mm) needles. Work 5 rows st st.

First row of picot edge: k1*, k2 tog, yo, repeat from* to end, finish k1.

Next row of picot edge: p.

Work 5 rows st st. The hem is now completed.

Change to reverse st st until work measures 11½ inches (29 cm) from picot holes. Divide work, leaving 68 sts for back and 33 sts for each front.

Work on right front stitches (33) only, using a second set of needles, knit 33 st then cast off 4 sts at armhole edge on next row.

Cast off 1 st at armhole edge on alternate rows five times (24 sts left). Continue on these 24 sts until front measures 6¼ inches (16 cm) from armhole.

Cast off 4 sts at neck edge.

Cast off 1 st at neck edge every alternate row, four times.

Continue on these 16 sts until work is 3 inches (7.5 cm) from cast off neck edge.

Next row, starting at neck edge, p 8 sts, turn and knit these 8 sts just worked, then work two rows across all stitches. Leave 12 inches (30.5 cm) of yarn, break the rest, and put stitches on a holder.

15. Almost woven in appearance, this genuine Shetland waistcoat was made from one gingery-brown (moorit) fleece from this rare breed

This method of shaping the shoulders sometimes results in a hole which is visible when a smooth, even yarn is used, but does not show on a textured yarn.

Complete left front to match.

Complete back using the same decreasings for the armholes as the fronts. The back neck is cast off leaving 16 sts on needles at each shoulder.

Graft right and left shoulder seams using sts on holders.

The front and neck edge are finished with a turned back picot hem worked in the same way as the bottom edge of the waistcoat.

66 sts are picked up on each front.

70 sts are picked up round the neck edge.

Two rows of a double crochet stitch give a neat, firm edge to the armholes.

Slip st at the picot edges into place (the row of holes forms a serrated edge).

Make a 4/6 stranded cord and thread through neck edge and finish with a small tassel at each end.

6 Crocheted jacket with felted and embroidered panel

This unusual jacket (fig. 1b and colour plate 2) incorporates various skills: spinning, crocheting, embroidery and felting. Feltmaking is a textile process which has been employed for thousands of years, and is now enjoying something of a revival in popularity with artists and craft-workers. It is a valuable skill for the handspinner to acquire because felted panels can often be combined to great effect in handspun articles. It's also an interesting and alternative way of hand-crafting from the raw material every spinner has. Many fibres will felt, but wool is the best and most widely used.

Under pressure, wool fibres will 'creep' in a root-to-tip direction. This tendency and the fibre's natural elasticity cause the mass of fibres to become entangled, forming a homogenous layer of felt. Warmth and moisture from weak alkali solutions speed the felting process. Finer wool fibres with more crimp and scales felt much easier

16. Heavyweight, indigo-dyed jacket with unusual felted panel

than coarser ones. Different types of wool produce noticeably different felts: some are smooth
and firm, others soft and hairy. It's fun experimenting with fleeces fom various breeds.

Methods of feltmaking vary, but all have four
common elements: heat, moisture, pressure and
chemical help. Originally, my chosen method
involved rolling layers of wool in muslin or
sheeting and squeezing along the roll until it
felted. The big disadvantage of this method is that
you can't see what is happening.

Not much has been published on the subject,
and I could find little information of practical
help. It was a case of learning the hard way – a
painful experience which on one occasion resulted in skinned hands. Eventually I discovered
what I think is the best method and one which
enables you to watch and control the process. For
this reason, I describe it in some detail in the
context of making this jacket.

To determine how a particular type of wool will
behave during felting, a sample square should be
made, so that you can calculate and allow for
shrinkage. Each time you use a different type of
wool, make a note including the amount of
shrinkage and pin it to the sample square.

For the jacket, I made my sample square from
Texel wool. This breed originates from the island
of Texel, off the North West coast of Holland. It
was imported to Britain, from France, in 1971.
The wool is highly crinkled, fine and has an
average staple of 3 to 5 inches (8 to 13 cm). It has
a Bradford count of 56 and average fleece weight
is $6\frac{1}{2}$ lbs (3 kg).

First, I cut a 10 inch (25 cm) square of thick
polythene from a carrier bag. This acts as a guide,
the difference between the finally-shrunk felt
piece and the polythene square being the amount
of shrinkage. My test piece shrank one and a half
inches (4 cm) all round, so for a 20 inch (51 cm)
square felted panel, for example, on the finished
garment, you would have to allow 3 inches (8
cm) for shrinkage.

Either washed or greasy wool may be used, first
carded by hand or on a drum carder. Careful
hand carding is adequate for most projects,

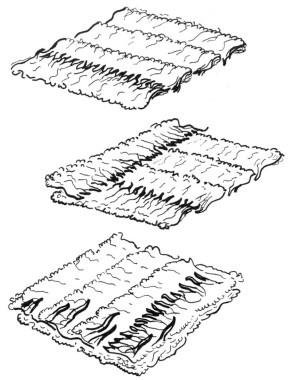

17. Arrangement of hand-carded webs and purple
locks for test square

although a drum carder is a great time-saver,
especially for the bigger jobs. Thorough carding is
essential because you need to build up even
layers. For the sample square, take four unrolled
carded webs and lay them alongside each other,
overlapping them slightly to compensate for the
differences in thickness. Then do the same with
four more, laying this second layer on top of and
at right angles to the first layer. For special effect
on the felted panels of my jacket, I placed a few
teased-out locks of elderberry-dyed Texel on top
(fig. 17)

Now make the felting solution in a jug, using a
heaped tablespoon of soap flakes (or liquid soap)
and a level tablespoonful of washing soda to a
litre of boiling water. The polythene pattern is
placed under the layers of wool and a little of the
soap solution poured evenly on top, taking care
not to wet the wool too much. Some people wear
lightweight plastic or rubber gloves, but I prefer

to feel my work and gloves sometimes cause the wool to stick to them. Starting at the centre, pat the wool down gently to get rid of the air. When all the air has gone and the square is wet and soapy, start rubbing very gently at first in small circles, always beginning at the edges. If you rub from the centre outwards then the work will soon get bigger than the pattern and too thin.

Great care is needed at first, otherwise the layers will be disturbed and thin patches or loose bits will result. After rubbing for a few minutes, I pat the work with my hand, gently at first. Continue rubbing and patting, gradually increasing the pressure until the wool begins to felt. If it starts spreading beyond the pattern I encourage it back by more circular rubbing at the edges. As the solution gets cool, squeeze out and add more liquid. If the work becomes too wet, the fibres will not mesh together but simply swim or slide past each other and you will spend hours wrestling with a soggy mess. Too much soap will have the same effect. Knowing just how much soap solution or hot water is needed as a lubricant comes with practice; meanwhile too little liquid is better than too much.

As soon as one side starts to felt, I turn the square over and repeat the process – rubbing, patting, squeezing the cooled liquid out and adding either more hot soap solution or hot water. Test to see if felting is completed by pinching and lifting a few fibres. If they come away, more rubbing is needed. Test in several places until the fibres hold and you can lift the entire square.

You are now ready for fulling, a process which will shrink the felt and make it strong and firm. You can buy specially made ridged plastic boards or alternatively use an old washboard or even the kitchen sink drainer. Warm the board with hot water and add a little soap for lubrication. The felt is fulled by rubbing it backwards and forwards across the ridges, adding more liquid if necessary, until it will shrink no more. The direction in which you rub it over the ridges determines the direction the felt will shrink. If I am making a shaped article then I rub more in certain direc-

tions to achieve the desired shape. After fulling, the felt is rinsed thoroughly and dried. I use a spin dryer, reshaping the piece if necessary.

The sample for my jacket was firm and strong. Those elderberry-dyed locks had spread into attractive swirling shapes. But instead of bright purple, they were a drab grey colour. I had forgotten that soap affects some natural dyes! I decided that the felt for the jacket should be thicker than the sample, so an extra layer of carded wool would be needed. I used 14 ounces (400 g) of white Texel for the three layers, remembering to alternate the direction of the webs, and placed $\frac{1}{2}$ ounce (14 g) of blue indigo-dyed Texel on top. The polythene pattern measured 47 by 18 inches (119 by 46 cm) which, based on the test square, I calculated would give me a piece of felt 40 by 15 inches (102 by 38 cm) allowing for shrinkage and the trimming of uneven edges.

In order to get such a large piece of felt to full uniformly I had to remember which parts had been rubbed and make sure I rubbed in the same direction right across the felt. After rinsing and drying, I noticed that although most of the indigo-dyed wool had formed interesting patterns, two of the locks had not fully felted into the white wool, but hung loose. I spun some indigo-dyed wool and used the yarn to embroider round these two 'stray' locks.

The result was so visually effective that I decided to embroider the outlines of other interesting shapes in the rest of the piece. This led me to embroider small groups of flowers, clusters of French knots and areas of small circles made with running stitches. The stitchery was done with two shades of indigo-dyed yarn and some white Texel. Although the piece of felt was quite firm, when held against strong light one or two thinner sections could be detected. I backed the entire piece with lightweight iron-on interfacing and then trimmed the uneven edges.

The yarn for the crocheted upper half of the jacket was spun from Texel and white Jacob fleece. Despite yellowish stains on some of the wool, it dyed uniformly and successfully with

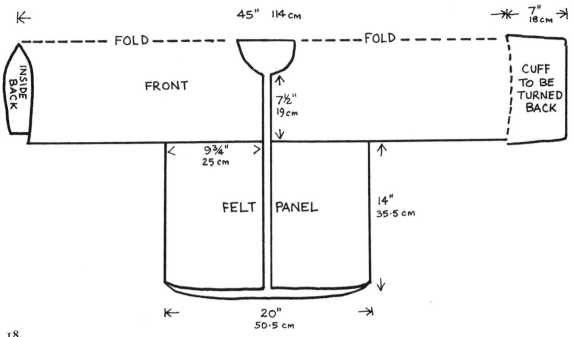

18.

indigo. When rinsed and almost dry, the wool was well teased out before carding. I find it much easier to tease wool when it is slightly damp.

I spun a medium-weight singles yarn on a jumbo flyer with a low ratio (4.3:1) and it crocheted easily without setting the twist. About 20 ounces (567 g) of dyed wool was spun.

Using a double crochet stitch I began by making a foundation chain the width of my back, plus the length of two threequarter-length sleeves. The crocheted part was then completed as shown in fig. 18. The two sections of the jacket were sewn together with indigo-dyed yarn using a backstitch, matching the centre backs and armholes on the crocheted top and the felt.

The top was stretched slightly to fit the felt and sewn with the crocheted edge overlapping the felt by $\frac{1}{4}$ inch (7 mm). As the felt edge formed the lower part of the armhole, no cutting was necessary. The sleeve seams were then stitched. An ounce (28 g) of finer yarn was spun and

19.

crocheted (using double crochet stitch) into a border to give a neat finish to the edges. The wide turned-back cuffs gave me the opportunity to use up almost all the remaining yarn. Rather than weigh the wool for each sleeve, I used a wool winder. This enables you to crochet both sleeves simultaneously by taking one end from inside the ball and the other from the outside, working for a few inches on alternate sleeves until nearly all the yarn has gone. Leave enough to make a tie cord for threading through the neck band.

Finally, a rectangular piece of lining material was sewn to the interfacing of the felt section.

7 Felt hats

Not only is this project an excellent opportunity to use up small quantities of fleece, but it can also add that important finishing touch to a handspun outfit. A knitted or crocheted jumper or jacket looks really special when it is worn with a felt hat of the same fleece (see page 41). A hat and a handspun scarf makes an unusual gift. Once the feltmaking technique is mastered, a hat can be made in about an hour.

Before tackling hats you should practice feltmaking with flat pieces (as described in the previous project). Making a hat is then relatively easy and, using the same technique, you can also produce articles like mittens and bootees. A pattern for a woman's brimmed hat is shown in figure 20. This polythene pattern allows for average shrinkage, but obviously the measurements will depend on which type of fleece you use. To arrive at a pattern for the size you require, follow the procedures detailed above.

For a hat to match my crocheted jacket with felted panels I dyed with indigo about 5 ounces (150 g) of Texel wool. Divide the wool into four piles and card each one. To make the front of the hat take two webs or layers of the carded wool and place them in such a way that one layer is horizontal and the other vertical – the horizontal layer being used on the outside of the hat to add strength. Place your pattern on top.

Now carefully tear the wool around the pattern, allowing an extra inch (2.5 cm) to allow for

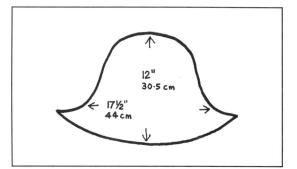

20. Pattern for hat with a brim

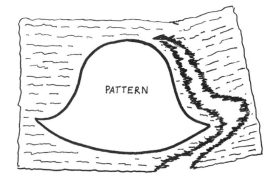

21. Tear the wool carefully to the pattern shape, allowing an extra inch (2.5 cm) for seams

the seam (fig. 21). To make the back of the hat, do exactly the same. Make up a litre of felting solution. Lay one half of the hat right side down

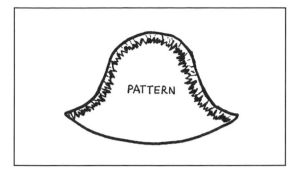

22. Place pattern on wet hat half and fold over the dry seam allowance

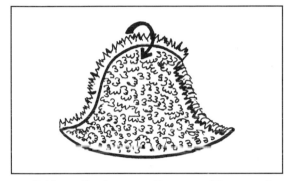

23. Fold over the dry seam allowance of the second half onto the first hat half

(vertical layer uppermost). Pour on one third of the felting solution, but be careful not to wet the 1 inch (2.5 cm) seam allowance, except at the bottom or brim edge. Pat the wool to get rid of the air. Neaten the brim edge by turning up 1 inch (2.5 cm). Place the pattern on top of the wet wool and fold the dry edges over it (fig.22). Place the other half of the hat on top, right side (horizontal layer) uppermost, and follow the same steps as for the first half of the hat, ensuring that when you turn up the brim edge you do not envelop the pattern. Pat the wool to get rid of the air. Gently turn over the hat and fold the dry seam allowance over the first half – you may need more solution for this (fig. 23)

Felt both sides of the hat. Then turn it inside-out and continue felting, paying special attention to the side seams, removing the pattern after a while. During fulling, the hat is rubbed in all directions first of all. To shape the crown, put your hand inside the hat and rub in all directions.

Whilst fulling, keep trying on the hat so you can tell which parts need more shrinking. I keep a thin sheet of polythene handy to protect my hair. Always remember that whichever way you rub is the way your hat will shrink, i.e. lengthways or widthways. If the brim is uneven, trim it and put it back on the board for more fulling. This will give a rounded edge to the brim rather than a square cut – which is what you would get if you trimmed the finished hat.

When you are satisfied that the hat is the right shape and size, it should be rinsed and spin-dried. Pull it into shape (or use a form) and dry.

You may like to try making hats of various styles and shapes. It's also interesting to experiment with different types of wool: some wools produce a soft, hairy felt (e.g. a good Welsh fleece) and a lovely floppy hat, while others (like Southdown or Merino) make a firmer felt suitable for a stiff-brimmed hat. A starch spray can also be used for a stiffer brim. You can use different colours for the brim and crown or the inside and outside of the hat.

Yet more variations are possible when the hat is finished off with a band or cord. For the hat described, I made a twisted cord by spinning left-over bits of carded wool. Other hats have had bands made up from scraps of felt, sewn on or simply tied in a knot. A knitted or crocheted band of handspun yarn to match also looks good, as do rows of stitching round the brim.

8 Jacket with bands of woven braid

The distinctive feature of this jacket (fig. 24) is the way that bands of woven braid are used. The bodice is made up of six strips of knitting which are then gathered and sewn on to the braid. The simple technique of card or tablet weaving using handspun yarns is easily learned and the braid speedily woven. You can also carry it around with you: the average length of weaving slips easily into a handbag. I took mine on holiday and wove with the strip tied to a Grecian column. Handspinning a warp yarn suitable for card weaving is not something I would advise a novice spinner to attempt. Most books recommend using a commercial, tightly spun cotton yarn for learning this weaving technique – so you see it's quite a challenge to spin your own! There are several good books devoted to card weaving (see bibliography) so what follows is only a working outline of the method used for this jacket.

For the wavy patterned braid you will need 12 cards. These may be bought from a weaving supplier and are usually of plastic, or you can make your own quite easily from stout card or beer mats. I find beer mats ideal providing they are new. Old mats with bent corners are difficult to work with. It also helps if both sides of the mat are not identical in colour or design.

The cards should be $3\frac{1}{2}$ to 4 inches (9 to 10 cm) square, with rounded corners. Using an office punch, make a hole in each corner – not too close to the edge or the corner will be weakened. A larger hole in the centre of each card is useful but not essential. I made centre holes with a red hot poker. All the holes must be smooth so that the warp threads do not catch and wear unnecessarily. On one side of the card, mark each hole A, B, C, and D (fig. 26). An extra mark in one corner will help when checking the threading. Number your cards 1 to 12.

I wove the braid for the jacket in two strips, one longer than the other. You will find it easier to start with the shorter warp, which in this case was 75 inches (190 cm) long. After weaving and finishing it make a braid of 45 inches (114 cm). For this shorter warp you will need about $1\frac{1}{2}$ oz (43 g) of warp yarn and about $\frac{1}{2}$ oz (15 g) of weft yarn. For the longer strip of braid, I made a warp of 215 inches (545 cm) which gave me a finished braid of 164 inches (416 cm). For this you will need $4\frac{1}{2}$ to 5 oz (130 to 140 g) of warp yarn and about $1\frac{1}{2}$ oz (43 g) of weft yarn. For this pattern, the warp yarn is in the proportion of 20 white threads to 28 dark threads. All the weft yarn is dark and spun just as the dark warp yarn: the weft should always be the same colour as the outer warp threads to make the edge neat.

The fleece was soaked for a short time (essential when drum carding) and when dry was sorted. Short locks around the belly area were removed and the remaining wool sorted for colour, reserving the darkest bits for the braid. If using handcarders, you should make a semi-

24. Some $1\frac{1}{2}$ lb (650 g) of white and grey Jacob fleece
is used to spin yarn both for knitting and card
weaving the braid in this jacket

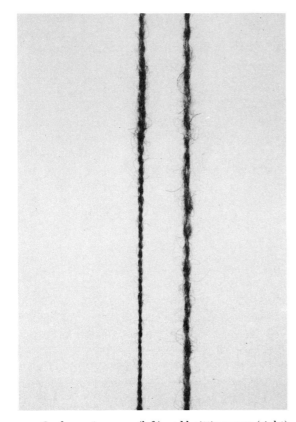

25. Card weaving yarn (left) and knitting yarn (right)

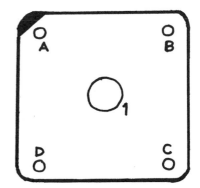

26. Beer mat card ready for weaving

worsted roll, not a rolag, in the way described on page 21.

Because the warp yarn has to withstand a tremendous amount of strain and friction, the staple length of the wool used must be at least $3\frac{1}{2}$ inches (9 cm). I spun a semi-worsted yarn on a single band wheel, with the drive band on the smaller flyer groove to give a 10.5:1 wheel ratio. Even with this higher ratio I needed to treadle quickly to get the right amount of twist for a strong yarn. Use the worsted draw technique, keeping your right (or front) hand in contact with the yarn at all times, controlling the twist and smoothing the yarn as you go. This technique enables you to pull the fibres from both ends as you draw, helping to straighten them, so avoiding a hairy yarn. The aim is to spin a smooth and even singles yarn with a high twist, which is then

plied. Because of the extra twist, take care when plying to avoid snarls in the yarn. Keep a good tension and if one of the singles begins to snarl, give it a sharp tug.

To wind the short warp, you will need two warping posts set 75 inches (190 cm) apart. Two pegs in the ground or two chairs will do the job. The warp yarn can be left on a lazy kate or wound into centre pull balls. Have ready about 36 inches (91 cm) of any contrasting yarn for use in tying groups of threads as the warp is made. Use the threading diagram (fig. 27) and, reading from left to right, begin with number 12 – which has four dark threads indicated. Tie the dark warp yarn to one peg, take it around the other peg and back (this makes two warp ends); repeat the trip and you have the four dark threads for number 12 card. Double the piece of contrasting yarn and loop it around this first group of threads (fig. 28) some 18 inches (46 cm) from one peg. Then put a chain round each sucessive group as the warp is made (fig. 29).

Card number 11 has the same warp threads as number 12, but when you get to number 10 the white yarn must be tied to one of the pegs. When not using a colour, loop the yarn round a peg, keeping the tension. When the warp is complete, tie one or two choke ties (firm ties to keep the threads together) and take the warp from the peg furthest from the coloured chain. Tie it in an overhand knot as near to the end as possible. Now take it off the other peg, being careful not to disturb the coloured chain, and cut right across

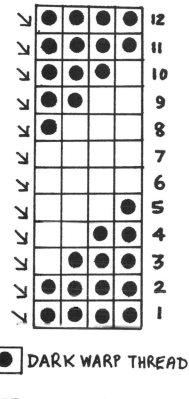

●	●	●	●		12
●	●	●	●		11
●	●	●			10
●	●				9
●					8
					7
					6
			●		5
		●	●		4
	●	●	●		3
●	●	●	●		2
●	●	●	●		1

● DARK WARP THREAD

☐ WHITE WARP THREAD

27. Threading diagrams for wave patterned braid

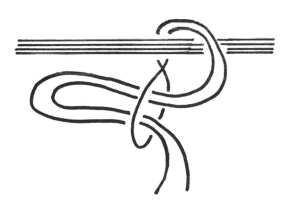

28. Starting knot for chain

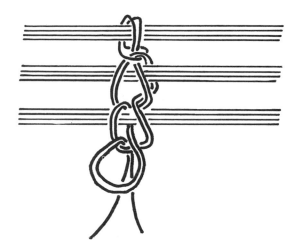

29. Chain completed over three groups of warp threads

the threads as near to the ends or loops as possible, giving an even bunch of cut ends ready for threading through the cards.

This is done with a crochet hook or bent wire. Spread the warp on a table with the cut ends towards you. Stack the cards face up in numerical order with no. 1 at the bottom and no. 12 at the top. The arrows on the threading diagram tell you which way to thread the cards. In this particular pattern, all warp threads are threaded downwards, i.e. going into the front and down the holes to the back. Thread each card in turn, finishing with number 1, then pull undone the coloured chain. Slide the cards up the warp just far enough to be able to tie an overhand knot, checking that the ends are as even as possible. Slip a pipe cleaner or shoelace through the centre holes to keep the cards in order. If you didn't make this hole, put an elastic band round the cards. Push a piece of cord through the overhand knot you have just made and tie to a chair back. The other end of the warp is tied in a similar fashion to a convenient door knob, tree or other suitable object. As the weaving grows, you will have to undo the cord and tie it again to bring the work nearer, eventually tying the braid itself to the chair back. Wind the weft into finger hanks or

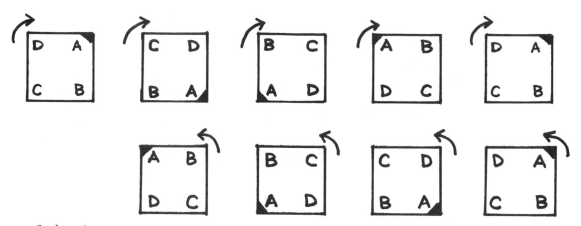

30. Card turning sequence

butterflies. Tension the warp by shuffling your chair until the threads are tight enough for the cards to turn cleanly but not so tight that the weft cannot be packed down easily.

Check that the cards are in the right order (from no. 12 on the left to no. 1 on the right) and that the marked sides of the cards all face to the right, with holes A and D at the top. With the pipe cleaner or rubber band removed, move all the cards towards you and then back again to clear the shed. You are now ready to start weaving: turning the cards easily is a knack soon acquired. Try to turn them firmly but gently together. Pass the weft through the shed leaving a 12 inch (30.5 cm) end which will be incorporated into a fringe later. Turn the cards clockwise (away from you) a quarter-turn and holes D and C will now be at the top (fig. 30).

Beat the previous weft in place with your fingers or a small ruler. Pass the weft back through the shed and then turn the cards another quarter-turn clockwise. Holes C and B will now be at the top. The sheds may not clear immediately, especially at first, but sliding them up and down the handspun warp should really be avoided. I use my hand to free any 'sticky' warp threads and if they are obstinate flick them with my fingers. You can see the advantage of a smooth, non-hairy warp.

If you suspect that a warp thread is in the wrong place after a turn, spread the cards gently between both hands to find the errant thread. Continue turning the cards as shown in fig. 30: four moves are clockwise (away from you) and then four are anti-clockwise. This releases the accumulated twist in the warp. These eight moves complete one pattern. The width and evenness of the braid is determined by how tightly and consistently the weft is pulled each time. My braid was $1\frac{1}{4}$ to $1\frac{1}{2}$ inches (3 to 4 cm) wide. Card woven braid is warp faced, so your weft threads must be pulled tight enough to be hidden by the warp. When joining a new weft thread, simply overlap the old; loose ends can be cut later.

Beware of interruptions: it's easy to forget whether the next move of the cards should be forwards or backwards, unless you have become familiar with the pattern. It helps if you keep by you a marker, flipping it over each time you change direction. When you have woven as near to the end of the warp as possible, undo the end knot and slip the cards off, tying an overhand knot at the end of the woven braid.

Wash the braid in warm water with soap flakes or detergent. After rinsing well, give it a short spin in a washing machine and hang to dry. If necessary, press it lightly.

To make the knitting yarn for the rest of the jacket, the remaining 18 oz (510 g) was blended to a uniform grey. Thorough blending is important because any dark or white streaks running

1. About a third of Teeswater fleece was used for the sheep in this tapestry of the breed (82 by 61 cm).

2. Crocheted and felted jacket, felted hat and loopy body warmer, all dyed with indigo.

3. Capes and coat woven on a simple, home-made nail loom.

4. Easy to make, this jacket combines simple weaving techniques and hand knitting.

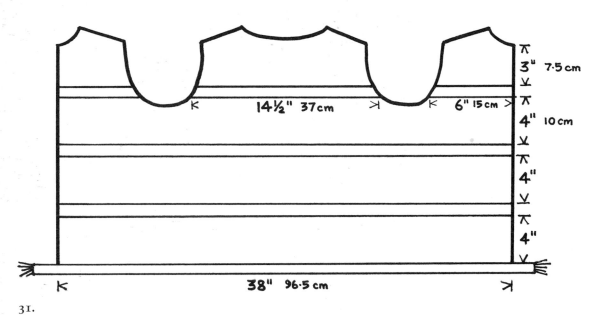

14½" 37cm   6" 15cm   3" 7·5 cm   4" 10 cm   4"   4"   38" 96·5 cm

31.

through the knitted sections would detract from the effect of the braid. If using hand carders, first tease and then blend the wool well. Achieving an even colour this way does need a lot of patience. Drum carders are ideal for blending and I used mine in the following way:

First carding   Teased wool placed on drum in roughly equal amounts of white and grey. Take each drum web and tear lengthways into three, putting each strip on a separate pile.

Second carding Take three strips from one pile at a time to make a new web. Tear each web into three as before and make three equal piles.

Third carding   Take three strips from one pile at a time. Resultant web should be uniform grey.

Carding the wool three times does not damage it if it is well teased beforehand, and if the wool is fed into the machine slowly and evenly.

The wool was spun using the long draw technique with a 10.5:1 wheel ratio on a single band wheel. If using a longer stapled wool you must draw the fibres back quickly making a yarn

which just holds together. Then treadle a couple of times at the end of the draw to achieve the right amount of twist before letting the yarn draw on to the bobbin. If you don't draw back fast enough, and the twist catches a group of long fibres they become very difficult to draw out, and a long slub is made in the yarn. The two singles were plied, making a yarn slightly finer and of course much softer (less twist) than that used for the braid. After washing and drying it was wound into centre pull balls for knitting.

PATTERN FOR JACKET

The size is 36 inches (91 cm) bust, but the pattern can be easily altered for other sizes by adding or subtracting a little more on the braid length and a few stitches more or less on the knitted sections. The number of stitches for the knitted portions is not critical to the fit because of the gathering.

The first, smaller piece of braid is used for the lower band with the tasseled ends left free, as in fig. 31. I used number 8 (4 mm) knitting needles. On a stocking stitch test square, 15 stitches gave me 3¼ inches (8 cm). For the gathering effect I used about half as much again as the required width. The first stocking stitch piece measured 60 by $4\frac{1}{2}$ inches (152 by 11.5 cm) using 280 stitches and weighed three oz (85 g).

I sewed the pressed, knitted strips to the braid as I went along. Place the braid a $\frac{1}{4}$ inch (0.75 cm) over the knitting and sew with a backstitch, gathering up the fullness. Make a $\frac{1}{4}$ inch turning on the two front edges.

Make the second knitted section in exactly the same way. Then cut a piece from the long braid measuring 41 inches (104 cm) – this allows $1\frac{1}{2}$ inches (3.5 cm) at each end for turning back – and oversew the cut edges by hand or use a zigzag stitch on a sewing machine, to prevent fraying.

The third knitted section is made as follows: cast on 280 sts and knit $1\frac{1}{4}$ inches (3.5 cm). Divide the stitches: 140 for the back and 70 for each front. Working on one front section only, cast off 7 sts at armhole edge. Decrease 1 st every alt. row at this edge seven times (56 sts). Continue straight until work measures $4\frac{1}{2}$ inches (11.5 cm) then cast off.

Rejoin wool to remaining front section and repeat armhole shaping. Join wool to middle 140 st and repeat armhole shaping at each end, i.e. leaving 112 sts after decreasing. The two top pieces of braid are each cut to 9 inches (23 cm) for the front and $17\frac{1}{2}$ inches (44.5 cm) for the back. This allows $1\frac{1}{2}$ inches (3 cm) for turnings.

The fourth knitted section has three parts and is made as follows:

Right front

Cast on 57 sts and knit $3\frac{1}{2}$ inches (9 cm).
Dec for neck edge – cast off 11 sts.
Dec 1 st at neck edge every row 8 times.
Start shoulder shaping – cast off 7 sts next row and P to end of row. *At the same time* continue with neck edge decreasing.
K 1 row.
Repeat these last two rows twice more.
Cast off remaining sts.

Left front

Work as right front, reversing the shaping.

Back

Cast on 116 sts.

Continue on st st for 5 inches (13 cm).
Cast off 7 sts then knit to end of row.
Cast off 7 sts then purl to end of row.
Repeat these last two rows.
Cast off 7 sts K 9, turn.
P 1 row.
Cast off 9 sts.
Break yarn and rejoin to middle section to cast off 30 sts. Join yarn to remaining stitches and shape left shoulder to match the right one.

Sleeves

These are elbow length and quite full. Each takes about 3 oz (85 g) of wool.
Cast on 110 sts.
Work $6\frac{3}{4}$ inches (17 cm) in st st.
Cast off 7 sts at the beginning of the next two rows.
Dec 1 st each end of every row until 34 sts remain.
Cast off 2 sts next 2 rows
Cast off 3 sts next 2 rows
Cast off 4 sts next 2 rows
Cast off 5 sts next 2 rows
Cast off remaining 6 sts.

Finishing

Press sleeves and sew underarm seams.

Placing right sides together sew shoulders together at edge using a running stitch. Pull to gather this up to the right length, $4\frac{1}{4}$ inches (11 cm) or your own shoulder width. Go over this row of stitching with a firm backstitch using a matching yarn. Sew sleeves to bodice, easing in a little fullness at the sleeve head. Cut two strips of braid each 13 inches (33 cm) (allowing 1 inch [2.5 cm] each end for the seam). Sew braid sections to make sleeve bands, and oversew to neaten the cut edges inside. Gather up lower edges of sleeves to fit braid and sew, overlapping braid $\frac{1}{4}$ inch (0.75 cm) as before. Cut a length of braid 20 inches (51 cm) for neck, allowing 1 inch each end for turning. Adjust the fullness of knitted sections and sew using a backstitch. Insert a 20 inch (51 cm) open-ended zip fastener, making sure the braid meets exactly at the zip opening.

9 Woven capes and coat

One of the simplest looms to make and use is a nail loom. It can be made easily at home from materials costing only a few pounds and enables the spinner to produce woven articles combining a variety of handspun yarns.

I wove two capes and a coat on my semi-circular nail loom (see colour plate 3). I chose a length of cape which would reach just to my wrists, so arm slits were not needed. A dashing, full length cape would have to be woven on a huge loom and, as weaving is carried out on the floor, plenty of houseroom. My loom was small and light enough to be carried from workshop to garden on warm summer days. This project is ideal for handspinners because the yarn can be spun to fit between the ever-widening warp gaps.

I made my loom from a sheet of $\frac{3}{4}$ inch (2 cm) chipboard measuring $73\frac{1}{2}$ inches by $36\frac{1}{2}$ inches (186 cm by 93 cm) and a bag of 2 inch (5 cm) galvanized clout nails – for this loom you need 270 nails. You could use ordinary nails or other types of wood. Both sides of the board were sealed with polyurethane varnish, but the one quick coat was not enough in my particular case: in my enthusiasm I took the loom outside bright and early before the dew had dried on the lawn. The tight warp and the damp brought up the loom sides slightly. But, even after this mistreatment, the board settled down and after a few days was flat once more.

To make the loom, start by making a mark halfway along one of the longer sides of the board. Then mark points at each side of the halfway mark, 7 inches (17.5 cm) distant. A 7-inch radius semi-circle is drawn on the board as a guide for the first row of nails. This can be done with a piece of string secured by a drawing pin to the halfway mark. Mark the string 7 inches away from the pin and to this mark hold a felt tip pen. Guide the pen with one hand whilst pressing on the pin with the other. In the same way, mark a larger semi-circle, starting about $\frac{1}{4}$ inch (1 cm) along the edge from the corner, as shown in fig. 32.

Just inside the smaller semi-circle I hammered in (deep enough to be held firmly) 46 nails evenly spaced, just over $\frac{1}{4}$ inch (1 cm) apart. Then, as shown in fig. 32, another row of nails is added opposite the spaces. This row should be just far enough away from the first to enable a yarn to be wound easily round both rows. Along the line of the large semi-circle 90 nails were hammered in about $1\frac{1}{4}$ inches (3.25 cm) apart. Should you decide to add more warp ends as the weaving widens, then another 89 nails will have to be hammered into the gaps (as there is a wider gap there is no need to offset them this time). This is better left until later however: it is less confusing if you first warp the loom with the 90.

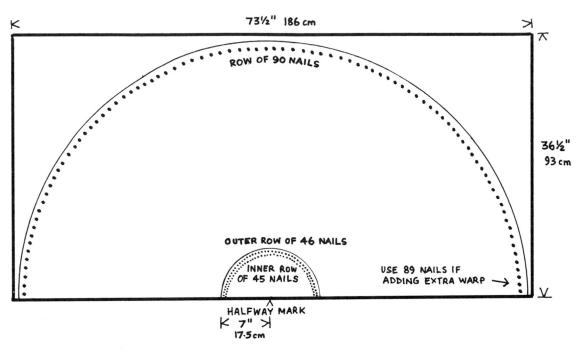

32. Cape or coat nail loom

COAT

Weight of warp: 6 oz (170 g)
Weight of weft: 3 lbs (1.36 kg)

This coat was woven first as a cape would be and then two slits were cut to make the side and sleeve seams. A small underarm gusset is darned in. This gusset is virtually invisible in a coat size 34 inch (86 cm) or 36 inch (91 cm) bust, but may be more noticeable in larger sizes. No extra warp threads were used. Instead, I relied on the increasing thickness of the handspun weft for a firm and closely woven fabric.

The two-ply warp was spun from a Masham fleece, but any wool with a staple of 3 inches (7.5 cm) or longer may be used. I spun a medium fine yarn on the smaller spindle groove of a jumbo flyer with a 9:1 wheel ratio. The disadvantage of a slight wobble when spinning a non-bulky yarn with an extra-large orifice on the wheel was overcome by having a large ball of warp with no knots. Spin the warp yarn with plenty of twist and as evenly as you can, remembering that the warp will be as strong only as its weakest point. It

doesn't matter if this warp yarn is hairy as there are no heddles or reed on which it could catch. I find it easier to warp the loom from a centre pull ball, although you may leave the yarn on a lazy kate.

Start to warp the loom by tying the yarn to the corner nail on the edge of the smaller semi-circle. Take the yarn to the first nail on the larger semi-circle, around this and back to the nail you tied on to. Make one more journey round these two nails because you need two extra warp threads at each edge to strengthen the selvedge. Now take the yarn round the first nail of the inner row of the smaller semi-circle and then up to the second nail of the larger semi-circle, as shown in fig. 33.

The warp should be tight, but not too tight. The natural tendency in warping a nail loom, especially at first, is to apply more and more tension as you go round the nails. If you didn't spin the warp on a large bobbin, tie a knot at one of the nails on the larger semi-circle. Finish the warp with a double set of warp ends on the last two nails.

This is a good project for using up odd batches of wool, and for the weft I used wool from many fleeces: Masham, Shetland, brown Suffolk and Texel. The cape was woven as a weft face, i.e. the weft completely covering the warp. If you want a lighter weight cape or don't have the 3 lbs (1.35 kilos) of wool needed for the weft, just pack the weft down gently, leaving some of the warp showing.

For the first few inches of weaving, it's easier to wind the weft into finger hanks or butterflies, and to beat it down with a kitchen fork. As the weaving progresses, you should wind the weft on to a small stick shuttle and pack it down with your fingers. The weaving position is a little uncomfortable and the work grows only slowly at first. But take heart, most of the cape is woven with thick weft and the weaving grows very quickly then.

The first weft was a fine singles Masham yarn spun with a 6.5:1 wheel ratio. This just covered the warp at the neck edge. Then the weft was gradually increased in thickness. After weaving about 14 inches (36 cm) the gaps between the warps had become quite wide so I switched to spinning with a jumbo flyer attachment and with a low wheel ratio of 4.3:1, giving a thick, very soft yarn which easily filled the gaps.

When you have woven to within a few inches of the nails, it gets a bit more difficult. You will only be able to take the shuttle under two or three warp ends at a time. In theory, you should be able to weave right up to the nails, push the weaving back slightly and slip the warp off the nails. I finished my cape about 1 inch (2.5 cm) from the nails. Because there were no knots in the warp, I decided to pull up the slack in each pair of warp ends from the inside of the cape, about 6 inches (15 cm) from the hem. A small overhand knot was tied and the remaining loop sewn back invisibly into the weft. At the neck edge, you will be left with a quite attractive row of small loops, or if you prefer turn back a small hem to the inside.

A 26-inch (66 cm) zip was sewn into the front. If you are not sure exactly which length of zip to

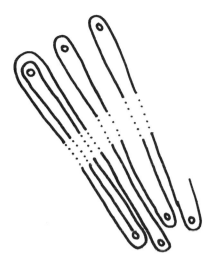

33. Path of warp on nail loom

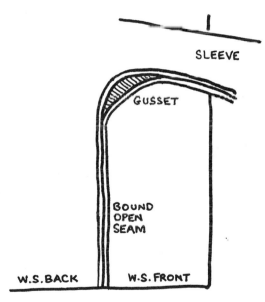

34.

buy, always choose the smaller size: a zip that is a little too long will tend to made the weaving buckle.

To make the cape into a coat, I cut two slits $12\frac{1}{2}$ inches (32 cm) from the front opening, making them 15 inches (38 cm) long. I bound all the edges with bias binding. Sew side seams of $11\frac{1}{2}$ inches (29 cm) and sleeve seams the same length, leaving a slit of around 9 inches (23 cm). It's wise to try on the coat at this stage so you can determine the width of the gusset. The widest part of my gusset measured $3\frac{1}{4}$ inches (8 cm). Matching yarn was used to darn the diamond shape, just as you would darn a sock, working from the outside so the bound edges remained inside, as shown in fig. 34.

MOHAIR AND SILK CAPE

Weight of first warp: $5\frac{3}{4}$ oz (163 g)
Weight of second warp: 3 oz (85 g)
Weight of mohair weft: 1 lb 10 oz (737 g)
Weight of silk weft: 4 oz (113g)

This cape was made from a creamy white mohair top (commercially scoured and combed) and a natural honey-coloured silk top. Although quite heavy, it hangs beautifully and is a lovely cape to wear on cool evenings in summer.

Mohair is the hair of the angora goat. It is a strong, silky, lustrous fibre. The first hair from the kid is the most prized because it is the finest. Each year the hair gets coarser.

Before spinning, the top must be broken into convenient lengths of around 12 inches (30 cm). If the top has been compressed, first spread the fibres out at the point where you want to break them and then pull apart. The fibres in my top averaged 6 inches (15 cm) in length, so needed little twist to make a good yarn. It is easy to overtwist mohair, making it almost rope-like. The best way of spinning any long fibre top is to hold a section over your right forefinger. Keep your finger in the centre of the fold and draw the fibres off the end like a funnel. I used a short draw worsted spinning technique, but instead of drawing the fibres forward with my free hand, drew them backwards with my right. My left hand controlled the twist.

For the plied warp yarn I used a 10.5:1 ratio on a single band wheel, but treadled slowly, allowing my right hand to pull back about 6 inches (15 cm) on each draw. The surface of mohair fibres is smooth, unlike wool with its cohesive scales, so after spinning a few feet (1 m) give the yarn a pull to test for strength. If it comes apart easily, you need more twist.

With the drive band on the larger spindle groove of my flyer, giving a 6.5:1 ratio, I could spin a softer twisted singles weft yarn. Without setting the twist, it was easy to weave with. If you prefer to weave with a balanced yarn, dip the hank in water and hang to dry, weighted.

Tussah silk, sometimes called wild silk, comes from silk worms which feed mainly on oak leaves, whereas Bombyx silk worms eat mulberry leaves. Tussah silk is coarser, stronger and not as lustrous as Bombyx or cultivated silk, but the colour ranges from pale grey to a deep honey brown. It is the tannin in the oak leaves that gives the silk these colours.

Because the silk fibres are so fine, it is easier to handle if the top is broken off lengthways and then divided into two or three small strips. The yarn is spun in a similar way to the mohair top, holding it lightly over your right finger, but this time drafting the fibres towards the wheel orifice with your left hand. I used a 6.5:1 wheel ratio to avoid overtwisting the singles yarn.

It is difficult to estimate the amount of shrinkage in silk. Some spun silk hardly shrinks at all, whilst others have been known to shrink by as much as 20 per cent. When weaving it with other fibres, it is important to pre-shrink the yarn. If you don't, the silk bands on the cape may pull in, resulting in an unattractive puckered effect when washing it for the first time. After hanking the yarn I left it in warm water for a few minutes. Following this brief soak I gave it a short spin (if it's warm outside I whirl it round a few times) and then straightened the hanks out with a couple of short tugs. It was then put to dry on an adjustable swift, set to a moderate tension, which had been covered with a piece of towel. If you don't have a swift, loop it over two chair backs.

Some experts recommend leaving the skein on a niddy noddy, spraying with water and leaving to dry. This process will set the twist, but in my experience will not pre-shrink the yarn for weav-

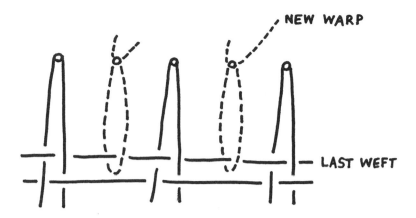

35. Adding a new warp, tying each pair individually

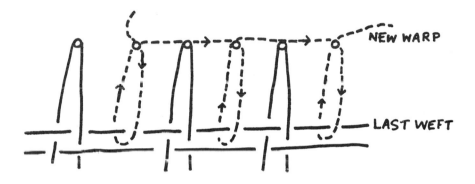

36. Adding a warp using long lengths of yarn

ing. Most people find it difficult to wind on to a niddy noddy loosely and you can't shrink a yarn which is held under strong tension.

The weaving started with a fine mohair weft. The first inch became weft faced because I pushed the weft firmly against the nails to give a neat neck edge. But soon I could make a more balanced weave (both warp and weft showing) by beating the weft in gently. After weaving about six inches (15 cm) I was using a thicker weft and decided to put in a band of silk. The silk was spun fine enough for me to beat it down into a weft faced weave, giving a solid 1 inch (2.5 cm) band of silk. I continued weaving with the mohair weft spun progressively thicker. Between

each silk band, lozenge shapes of silk were woven randomly. This distorts the silk bands and gives a scalloped appearance. Check that the silk bands meet exactly at the front edges however.

When 18 inches (46 cm) had been woven, the spaces between the warp threads were very wide, so I decided to add more warp threads. I hammered 89 nails into the spaces along the larger semi-circle. The new warp threads were looped over the last row of weft. There are two ways of doing this. One method is to cut the individual warp pairs and tie them on to each new nail, as in fig. 35.

Alternatively, cut the warp yarn to a convenient 3 or 4 feet (92 to 122 cm). Tie it on to the first new nail, loop it over the last woven weft thread, back to the first nail, around this, behind the next 'old' nail and on the second 'new' nail, as in fig. 36. When the length of warp runs out tie in a new length at a nail, and contine adding new warps right along the loom.

This is a much quicker method than the first as it does not involve tying so many knots. The skill in adding extra warps is to judge the tension correctly. As each new pair of warps is made, push the weft back into the weaving line and loop the warp round the nail with the same tension as the existing warp. If after weaving a few rows the new warp appears to loosen you can always adjust it by taking up the slack, and winding it one turn round a nail. After inserting new warps, the first three or four rows of weaving will be odd (you'll know what I mean when you do it) but then everything gets back to normal. Weave until 3 inches (7 cm) from the nails and before taking off the loom raise the nap on the mohair. This is best done with the work stretched out. Use a stiff hair brush evenly over the weaving. This really enhances the lustrous material.

After taking off the loom, the lower edge was finished by tying together each pair of warp ends at the hemline, and sewing them back invisibly into the weaving. Matching buttons were sewed on the front edge, opposite loops made from handspun silk yarn. I wear this cape with the fastening at my right shoulder.

WOOL CAPE

Weight of first warp: 6oz (170 g)
Weight of second warp: 3 oz (85 g)
Weight of weft: 1 lb 8 oz (680 g)

The warp yarn for his cape was spun from a St Kilda, or Hebridean, fleece. The remainder of the black fleece was used as weft at the top and bottom of the cape. I dyed some wool a dusky pink using a synthetic dye system in which I mixed the colours myself. This was spun into a singles weft yarn together with some grey Jacob wool, and some wool from a beautifully white Romney Marsh fleece. The colours were shaded gradually from one to another by adding the next colour in short lengths. I kept the next colour rolags by my main colour wool, and introduced them a few inches at a time, breaking off the main colour and then rejoining it. This cape is woven with a weft face, which uses more wool than a more open balanced weave, but it certainly keeps out the cold winter winds!

10 Alpaca top

This knitted top has wide cape sleeves and a deep ribbed welt. It is lovely to wear, being light yet warm, and the horizontal stripes emphasise the drape of this luxurious fabric.

The alpaca lives mainly in the South American Andes and resembles the llama, both animals being descendents of the camel. The alpaca's hair is long, crimpy, soft and silky. Its colour varies from white to bluish-grey and shades of brown to black. If regularly shorn, the hair grows 6 to 8 inches long (15 to 20 cm) each year, but if the animal is not clipped the hair can grow as long as 25 inches (63 cm). Yarns spun from alpaca are soft, dense and very warm, especially when the surface is brushed.

Alpaca became well-known in Britain because Sir Titus Salt of Bradford built up a thriving textile business based on producing alpaca cloth for the fashion houses. Queen Victoria kept two alpacas at Windsor Park and in 1844 sent their fleeces to Sir Titus to be made into his famous cloth. As his business expanded, Sir Titus decided to move his mill and all his workpeople out of congested Bradford to cleaner, better surroundings in the nearby valley of the River Aire. He built a 'model' village around the new mill for his employees. Saltaire took 20 years to complete and included houses, villas, schools, a shopping area, a church, bath houses, a hospital, alms houses, an institute building, a Sunday School and even a four-acre park on the banks of the River Aire.

Today, the 'alpaca village' of Saltaire is still an impressive place and attracts many visitors. I bought some inexpensive waste Alpaca top in two natural shades: instead of being in a continuous length it was cut bluntly in lengths which varied from $3\frac{1}{2}$ to 8 inches (9 to 20 cm) – some waste! Fibre length varied up to 6 inches (15 cm) so I decided to blend it all first by pulling apart and teasing the varied lengths together. Then it was carded into rolags. Had I bought a more costly full-length top, I would have spun it as a mohair top by holding a section of it over my right index finger. I spun my rolags using a short woollen draw on a 6.5:1 wheel ratio. The yarn needs just enough twist to hold it together and should be soft and fluffy. Two single yarns were plied.

The following pattern is for a 32 to 36 inch (81 to 91 cm) bust. For a larger size, add more stitches initially and work a few more rows before starting the shoulder shaping. I had plenty of mid-brown alpaca and only a little of a darker, chocolate shade, so I made random stripes (making a note of them so I could produce the 'random' striping on the back piece).

PATTERN

Back and front alike.
Tension: $5\frac{1}{2}$ stitches to 1 inch (11 stiches to 5 cm)
$7\frac{1}{2}$ rows to 1 inch (15 rows to 5 cm)

37. To make this top you will need 11 oz (300 g) of
alpaca in two shades.

desired, until there are 199 sts.

Shoulder shaping: Dec 1 st at each end of next 3 rows.

Work 1 row straight.

Rep these last 4 rows until 151 sts remain.

Neck shaping: K2 tog, K59, cast off next 30 sts, K to last 2 sts, K2 tog.

Continue on last stitches only.

Dec 1 st at each end of next 7 rows.

Dec 1 st at shoulder edge only on every row until 34 sts remain.

Work 1 row.

Cast off 4 sts.

Rejoin yarn to neck edge of remaining stitches and work this side to match.

When both pieces are finished, pin out the stocking stitch sections to shape and steam lightly with an iron – never actually touching the knitting, and then brush with a hairbrush whilst the work is still slightly damp. When dry, join one shoulder seam. With the right side facing, pick up 146 sts round neck with number 10 ($3\frac{1}{4}$ mm) needles and knit two rows, decreasing one st each row. Cast off. Join the other shoulder seam. With number 10 ($3\frac{1}{4}$ mm) needles pick up 160 sts on each sleeve edge, beginning at the top of the ribbing, working over the shoulder, and back down to finish at the other ribbing. Work two rows then cast off. Join the rib seams.

Never put an iron directly on to alpaca fabric, because the fibres compress easily and the fluffy texture of the yarn can be damaged. If your alpaca top gets creased, treat it as you would wool: hang it somewhere warm and if possible steamy (a bathroom is ideal) and any creases should soon drop out.

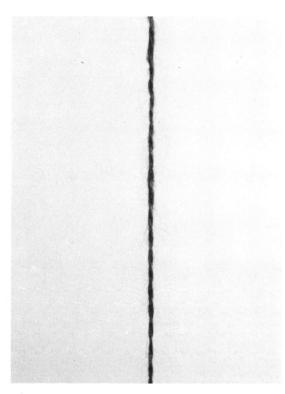

38.

With no. 10 ($3\frac{1}{4}$ mm) needles cast on 94 stitches.

Work 5 inches (13 cm) of knit 2, purl 2 rib.

Increase in next row – rib 6* inc in next st, rib 7, repeat from* nine times, inc in next st, rib 7 (105 sts).

Change to no. 8 (4 mm) needles and continue in st st.

Inc 1 st at each end of next 2 rows.

Work 1 row straight.

Repeat these 3 rows, making bands of colour as

11 Linen table mat

One of the earliest fibres to be spun was flax. Fragments of linen yarn have been found in Turkey which date back to 6000 BC. Linen yarn is spun from the fibres of the flax plant Linum usitatissimum which remain when the outer bark and inside pith have rotted and been broken away. Flax is grown in Northern France, Belgium, Holland, Eastern Europe and Russia. Ireland produces the greatest amount of linen cloth in Europe, whilst Belgium and Holland are said to produce the finest quality fibre.

Unlike wool, you don't need a field to cultivate flax. Just a small plot of garden will suffice because the seeds are sown very close together – about 2,500 per square metre – to produce tall, straight, unbranching plants with attractive blue flowers. Growing flax is relatively easy, but the processes involved in making the fibres suitable for spinning are more complicated and time-consuming. These processes, with evocative names like rippling, retting, breaking and hackling, coupled with the pleasure of growing your own fibre, are felt by many handspinners to be well worth the effort involved.

One of my friends grew flax from seeds in a parrot feed mixture, cultivating it in a tiny back garden. The most difficult process, that of retting, was done in an old bath. Although some of the stalks in the bath had been allowed to rot too far (retting involves rotting), he ended up with some 4 oz of spun yarn. Undaunted, he harvested another crop the following year and, with the benefit of experience, produced much better results.

Good flax fibres are fine, strong, lustrous and smooth. They range in colour from a pale, yellowish white to shades of honey and grey. Linen does not shrink, repels dirt, absorbs and evaporates moisture quickly, but has little elasticity, so it wrinkles easily.

Three different forms of flax are available for the handspinner: tow, a commercially combed sliver, and line. Tow fibres are coarse and short because they are discarded fibres from the hackling process, but they can be combed and spun worsted fashion. Tow is not as strong as line, and if used for a warp is usually plied to add strength and reduce the effects of abrasion from heddles and reed.

Flax sliver, prepared for commercial spinning, has the fibres cut to around 4 inches (10 cm). Sometimes, it has an artificial crimp put in it, which later disappears, to make it technically suitable for machines designed for spinning wool. This sliver can be handspun, using a worsted draw, keeping your fingers damp to obtain a smooth yarn.

Flax line is preferred by handspinners. In this form, the fibres remain intact, but because they are anything from 20 to 30 inches (50 to 75 cm) long, require special preparation. Flax line is sold in bundles, called stricks. For the very finest

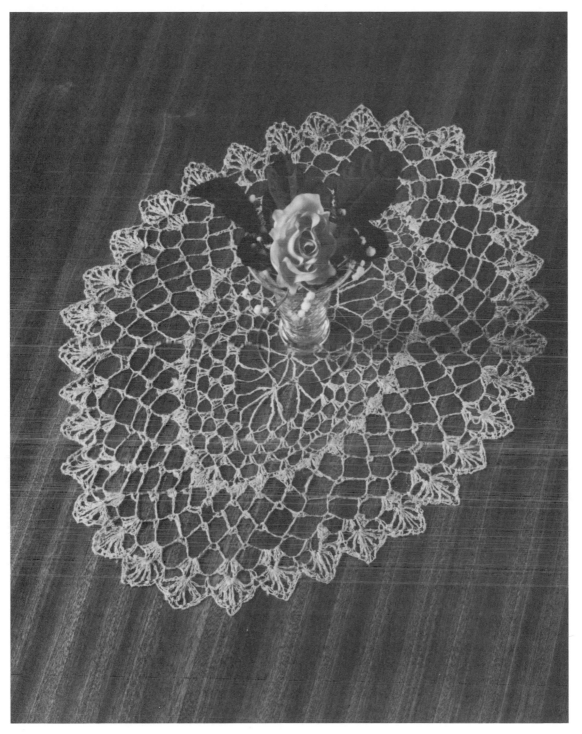

39. For a linen table mat like this, you will need $\frac{3}{4}$ oz (22 g) of flax

spinning, the strick is sometimes divided into three and only the middle portion used. The rest is considered uneven in fibre length and strength and the root part woody and coarse. Sometimes the inner fibres of the stalk are reserved for a fine yarn, as these are usually finer and whiter.

If possible, choose fibres with the project in mind: flax can be coarse and brittle or fine and supple. Many a handspinner, thinking 'flax is flax', has been discouraged because the strick bought was totally unsuitable for the fine, lace weight yarn needed. The first flax I spun was a very coarse, dark grey fibre and the yarn made an ideal rug and wall-hanging warp. It must have been from an old batch of stricks judging by the odd, pungent smell, which I thought all flax fibres must have, because some time later I encountered a delightful, fine and lustrous Belgian line which not only produced a fine and smooth yarn but smelled just like new-mown hay! So if you can, examine the strick before buying. Pinch out three or four fibres and hold them in your right hand, Lick the finger and thumb of your left hand and then roll the fibres in an anti-clockwise direction. This will give you a good guide to the finest yarn that can be spun from that particular strick.

Don't try to spin from a strick held on your knee: the fibres may quickly become a tangled mass. The best way to control these long fibres properly is to use a distaff. It's possible to improvise with a broomstick, positioned some 2 feet (60 cm) higher than the spinning wheel orifice. I have an old flax wheel with a lantern distaff, but for a modern wheel, an arrangement as shown in fig. 40 works admirably. A 1 inch (2.5 cm) piece of wood dowelling is set into a small bracket, screwed to the wheel at a convenient spot near the front. A piece of wood 7 by $1\frac{1}{4}$ inches (17.5 by 3 cm) with two holes – one for the distaff dowelling the other to fit on the bracket – enables the distaff to swivel. For a standard Ashford wheel, the distaff dowelling measures 34 inches (86 cm) to give the required 24 inches (61 cm) above the orifice.

With a shaped distaff the prepared fibres can go

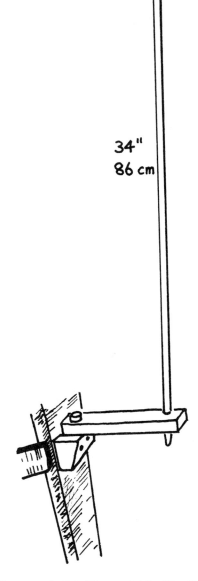

40. Home-made distaff for an Ashford Traditional wheel

34"
86 cm

straight on, but with dowelling or similar, you'll need to make a paper cone shape. I use screwed up newspaper or tissue paper to build up the cone shape around the pole, fastened with sticky tape. Then a smooth outline is made with a few uncrumpled sheets, again securing with sticky tape.

Some imperfectly prepared stricks have straw-like bits, called boon, sticking to the fibres. If so, the strick will have to be rehackled. This can be done with a metal dog comb or a strong plastic comb with wide spaces between the teeth. Holding the strick in the middle, start combing at one end, gradually working your way to the middle. Then turn the strick round and repeat the process. The fibres caught in the comb can be spun later as tow.

A strick that is free from boon just needs two firm shakes, holding it tightly first at one end and then the other. Carefully separate $1\frac{1}{2}$ to 2 oz (40 to 60g) from the strick. This will be enough to dress the distaff. You need a cloth to fit over your knee or, if you prefer to work standing, place it on a table; a piece of string or tape about 40 inches (100 cm) long and $2\frac{1}{2}$ yards (228 cm) of $\frac{3}{4}$ to 1 inch wide ribbon. Tie the middle of the tape about 3 inches (7.5 cm) from the root tip of the small strick. The fibres are more together at the root end and tend to be coarser and woollier than at the flower tips, which have finer and more uneven fibres. Place the cloth over your knee, fasten the tape to your waist with the strick to your middle. Now hold the strick as near to the tip as possible in your left hand, arm outstretched towards your right side. Give the strick a little shake to encourage a few fibres to loosen. If they refuse to fall on to your lap, pat a few down with your right hand, as shown in fig. 41.

Once the fibres begin to fall, move the strick slowly to your left side, leaving a fan-shaped trail of criss-cross fibres. The right hand is used for patting down any fibres as necessary. The fibres should fall down evenly, but only a few at a time and never radiating in a straight line from your waist otherwise they will not draw down properly later. When you reach the far left-hand side

of the cloth, change to holding the strick with the right hand. The left hand is now used, palm down, for patting the fibres as they are released. Move the strick over to your right (fig. 42) making a second fan-shaped web, and change hands again. Continue in this way until all the strick lies on your lap. Aim for many fine layers rather than fewer and thicker ones and the distaff will be better dressed and easier to spin from.

Remove the tape from around the waist, carefully scooping up the cloth without disturbing the fibre arrangement and lay it on a floor or table. Untie the knot holding the root end. Place the top of the prepared distaff at the point where the tape tie was and at one edge of the fan shape (fig. 43). Gently roll the distaff round the flax, keeping the distaff top at the apex of the fan shape, tucking up any stray fibres as you roll. Where the two ends meet, pat down carefully to make a neat join. Now tie the middle of the ribbon to the top of the distaff, to hold the strick firmly, and cross it several times around the cone shape, finishing off with a bow (fig. 44).

Place the distaff in its holder, with the lowest fibres higher than the wheel orifice. Fluff up and spread out the plume of fibres above the tie.

Traditionally, the colour of the flax ribbon indicated the marital status of the spinner. Green or blue was used by a married woman, whilst an unmarried spinner had a red or pink ribbon. A newly dressed distaff is a lovely sight, and it's easy to understand why flax was preferred to wool by nineteenth-century women of leisure in their drawing rooms.

Looked at under a microscope, flax has an irregular surface and it is these irregularities which help the fibres to be spun into a cohesive yarn. Flax is spun in an anti-clockwise direction (S-twist) because this follows the spiral cellular structure of the fibres. The ancient Egyptians must have discovered that flax naturally twists anti-clockwise when wet, as their flax yarns were spun with an S-twist. If spun dry, the yarn would be quite rough and hairy, so flax is always spun wet with the moistened fingers smoothing any hairs back into the yarn.

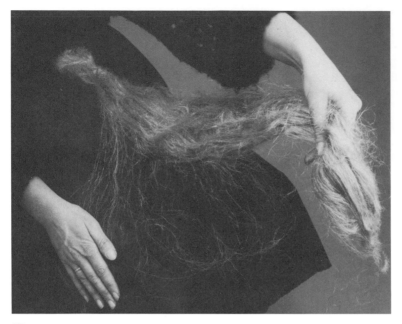

41.

42.

43.

Traditionally the fingers were moistened with saliva, hence references in old books to foul-mouthed flax spinners. More hygenically inclined spinners had little water pots, often made of pewter, set into their wheels or a small bowl hung near the distaff. I hang mine on the wheel.

There are two ways of spinning flax: a two-handed method or one using mainly only one hand. The first is the easiest to master. Tie a piece of S-twist or plied yarn on to the bobbin as a leader thread. You need slightly more twist for flax than the equivalent wool yarn, but to begin with treadle slowly with a low wheel ratio and little pull in tension in order to give your hands enough time to cope with a new spinning technique. Draw down a few fibres from the bottom of the distaff with your left hand and allow the twist from the leader thread to catch on to these. Moisten the fingers and thumb of the right hand and guide the spun yarn into the orifice. The right hand is now used for controlling the twist and smoothing and rolling the yarn. The yarn is lightly rolled between the thumb and fingers as the hand moves towards the distaff.

The left hand controls the fibre supply, pulling new fibres downwards, not forwards, with a stroking action, palm downwards. You have to remember that it is difficult, if not impossible, to draw back the fibres once the twist has entered because of their length. As the flax is spun from one part, the distaff is turned round so that the fibres are used evenly from all sides. The ribbon is retied as the flax is used up. When spinning a fine flax yarn, it is advisable to move the yarn not from one hook to the next but to the hook furthest away so that the thread lies diagonally across the bobbin. This is a precaution against breakage, loss of yarn and subsequent wastage. If you have to cut some away to find the end, you need only waste that spun after the diagonal thread. A lost end can sometimes be forced free if you treadle furiously in the opposite direction to that in which you spun, but this won't work with a bobbin braked wheel.

English flax spinners of old used the one-handed method. The left hand does most of the work, drafting the fibres and controlling the twist. The right hand takes over briefly when the left fingers have to be re-dampened, or occasion-ally holds the fibres back if too many have been

44.

mats, but I chose to crochet a delicate, oval lacy mat. You don't need much yarn and the mat is quickly made, so it's an ideal project if you want to experience for the first time the beauty of working with this natural fibre.

PATTERN

I used a No. 12 (2.5 mm) crochet hook, which resulted in a 16 inch (41 cm) mat.

Commence with 6 ch, join with a ss to form a ring.

Row 1: 3ch, into ring work 2 tr 3 dtr 2 tr 3 ch 1 ss 3 ch 2 tr 3 dtr and 2 tr, 3 ch, 1 ss into first of 3 ch.

Row 2: 1 ss into each of next 3 sts, 6 ch, 1 tr into same place as last ss, * 2 ch, miss 2 sts, into next st work 1 dtr 3 ch 1 tr tr 3 ch 1 quad tr 3 ch 1 tr tr 3 ch and 1 dtr, 2 ch, miss 2 sts, (into next tr work 1 tr 3 ch and 1 tr) twice; repeat from * once more omitting 1 tr 3 ch and 1 tr at end of repeat, 1 ss into 3rd of 6 ch.

Row 3: 1 ss into next sp, 6 ch, 1 tr into same sp, * 3 ch, 1 dtr into next dtr, 3 ch, into next tr tr work 1 tr tr 3 ch and 1 tr tr, 3 ch and 1 tr tr, 3 ch, into next quad tr work (1 quad tr 3 ch) 4 times and 1 quad tr, 3 ch, into next tr tr work 1 tr tr 3 ch and 1 tr tr, 3 ch, 1 dtr, into next dtr, 3 ch, miss 1 sp, (into next sp work 1 tr 3 ch and 1 tr) twice; repeat from * once more omitting 1 tr 3 ch and 1 tr at end of repeat, 1 ss into 3rd of 6 ch.

Row 4: 1 ss into next sp, 3 ch, 2 tr into same sp, * 2ch, 3 tr into next sp; repeat from * ending with 2 ch, 1 ss into 3rd of 3 ch.

Row 5: 1 ss into each of next 2 tr and into next sp, 3 ch, 2 tr into same sp, (2 ch, 3 tr into next sp) 5 times, 2 ch, into next sp work 3 tr 3 ch and 3tr, (2 ch, 3 tr into next sp) 1 3 times, 2 ch, into next sp work 3 tr 3 ch and 3 tr, (2 ch, 3 tr into next sp) 7 times, 2 ch, 1 ss into 3rd of 3 ch.

Row 6: 1 ss into each of next 2 tr and into next sp, 3 ch, 2 tr into same sp, (2 ch, 3 tr into next sp) 5 times, 2 ch, into next sp work 3 tr 3 ch and 3 tr (2 ch, 3 tr into next sp) 1 4 times, 2 ch, into next sp work 3 tr 3 ch and 3 tr, (2 ch, 3 tr into next

drawn down. Draw some fibres from the bottom of the distaff with the moistened left hand and join to the leader thread. As the hand moves back towards the distaff the twist is released between the thumb and index finger and the yarn is smoothed as the finger and thumb slide along it. When drawing down, the twist is held back and the fibres are rolled (the thumb sliding towards the tip of the index finger) and because this is in the opposite direction to that in which the fibres are being twisted, it becomes easier to draft out just the right amount of fibres.

Leaving the yarn to dry on my bobbin, I found it supple enough to crochet straight from a ball. Some flax may need to be softened however and this is done by boiling it, in hank form, for about an hour with soap flakes. Use $\frac{3}{4}$ oz soap to 1 oz flax.

Many spinners use flax yarn for weaving table

sp) 8 times, 2 ch, 1 ss into 3rd of 3 ch.

Row 7: 1 ss into each of next 2 tr and into next sp, 3 ch, 2 tr into same sp, (2 ch, 3 tr into next sp) 5 times, 2 ch, into next sp work 3 tr 3 ch and 3 tr, (2 ch, 3 tr into next sp) 15 times, 2 ch, into next sp work 3 tr 3 ch and 3 tr, (2 ch, 3 tr into next sp) 9 times, 2 ch, 1 ss into 3rd of 3 ch.

Row 8: 1 ss into next tr, 3 ch, 2 tr into same place as ss, * 1 dc into next sp, into centre tr of next tr group work 3 tr 3 ch and 3 tr; repeat from * ending with 1 dc into next sp, 3 tr into same place as ss, 1 tr into 3rd of 3 ch.

Row 9: 3 ch, 1 dc into loop just made, * 7 ch, into next loop work 1 dc 3 ch and 1 dc; repeat from * ending with 3 ch, 1 dtr into last tr of previous row.

Rows 10 to 14: 3 ch, 1 dc into loop just made, * 7 ch, into next 7 ch loop work 1 dc 3 ch and 1 dc; repeat from * ending with 3 ch, 1 dtr into dtr of previous row.

Row 15: 3 ch, 2 tr into loop just made, * 3 ch, into next 7 ch loop work 3 tr 3 ch and 3 tr; repeat from * ending with 3 ch, 3 tr into next loop, 3 ch, 1 ss into 3rd of 3 ch.

Row 16: 1 ss into each of next 3 sts, 1 dc into same loop, * into next loop work (1 dtr, 1 ch) 7 times and 1 dtr, 1 dc into next loop; repeat from * omitting 1 dc at end of last repeat, 1 ss into first dc.

Row 17: 1 ss into next tr and into sp, 1 dc into same sp, * (3 ch, 1 dc into next sp) 6 times, 1 dc into next sp; repeat from * omitting 1 dc at end of last repeat, 1 ss into first dc. Fasten off.

Each time you launder the mat it will become softer and lighter in colour. But if you want a paler colour immediately, bleach the mat with a dilute solution of household bleach and ensure it is rinsed thoroughly afterwards. Flax benefits from being ironed when damp. Pressed on the right side, it may be 'polished' to a high sheen: pressed on the wrong side, it will be matt.

12 Woven fringed jacket

There's a myth that 16 inch (40 cm) looms can only be used for making things like table mats and scarves. The first thing I wove on my new small rigid heddle loom was a jacket, made up from two strips of fabric. Weaving on a small loom is easy and enjoyable; I wove with the loom on my knee, the warp beam supported by a small table. The warp yarns were prepared worsted fashion and the weft semi-worsted, using a Teeswater fleece. Its long crimped locks already had a fine lustre, which was richly enhanced by worsted spinning. Although the jacket is not a 'loom-shaped' garment, very little of the precious hand-spun cloth is wasted. Even the loom tie-on waste was made into an attractive fringe.

A worsted yarn comprises fibres lying parallel to each other. It is made from long wool fibres from 4 to 10 inches (10 to 25 cm) from which any short fibres (noils) have first been combed out. The yarn is usually plied, and it is spun keeping the parallel fibre arrangement and not letting the twist enter the drafting zone. A worsted yarn is smooth, strong, lustrous and hardwearing. The fibres are aligned in such a way that little air is trapped between them, so the yarn is not such a good insulator as its woollen yarn counterpart. When woven, worsted yarns remain distinct in the cloth and are not finished to give a felted or close-textured quality.

A true worsted yarn is made by combing the fibres between two wool combs. These combs are heavy and long-handled, usually with between four and eight rows of long sharp teeth. They must be warmed first, so that the oiled fibres glide easily past the teeth, or tines. One of the combs is fixed into a stationary base, or pad. After repeated combing from one comb to the other, the fibres are drawn off through a ring, known as a diz, to make a long sliver. This then has to be divided into strips so that all the fibres are mixed (planking) before being recombed and drawn off. The short fibres remaining on the combs may be carded later and woollen spun.

I have a pair of light wool combs with two rows of teeth and I confess to using them in the worsted preparation of my warp yarn. But because such combs are difficult to obtain and spinners will be more interested in methods they can use at home, I will describe another way of producing an 'almost worsted' yarn. For those who have wool combs, there is an excellent book on the subject by Peter Teal (see bibliography).

My 'almost worsted' yarn has long fibres lying parallel and most of the short fibres have been combed out. Semi-worsted is a term loosely used today and refers to a variety of yarns which may be made as follows:

1 The yarn may be worsted spun from a rolag. This spinning method involves exerting a pull at both ends of the drafting zone, forcing some of the fibres to straighten and lie parallel instead of

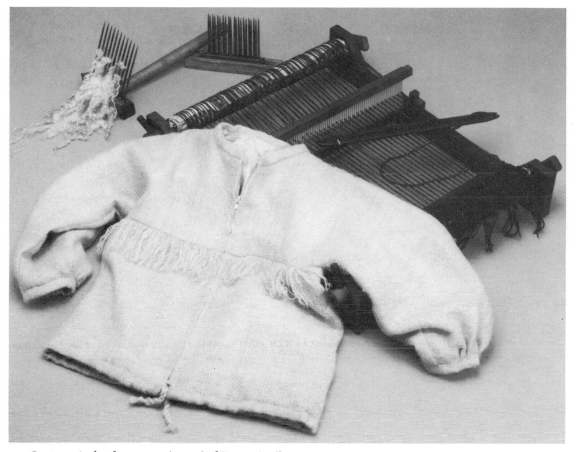

45. Lustrous jacket from 19 oz (540 g) of Teeswater fleece

being drawn from the rolag in a spiral formation (as when woollen spun). Only some of the fibres lie parallel in this yarn and the fibre lengths vary, giving quite a hairy yarn.

2 The yarn may be worsted spun from long fibre rolags which have been rolled acrosss the carder. This gives a more parallel fibre arrangement than from a conventionally rolled rolag, but the short fibres still remain.

3 A yarn can be made from teased fleece and worsted spun. Before teasing, check for straw etc. and second cuts. Hold the shorn end and open out the tips, turn the lock round and open out the cut end. This is a suitable method for a clean, freshly shorn, long stapled fleece as it can be spun in the grease. The yarn will have a parallel fibre

arrangement but the fibre length will vary considerably.

4 A yarn can be worsted spun from strips of a drum carded web. Drum carding does to some extent align fibres, especially if the locks are carefully teased and fed in end on. This yarn may have many fibres parallel, but short fibres are present too and tend to stick out of the yarn as it is being spun, giving it a rather fuzzy appearance.

5 A flick carder may be used to open up the staples before worsted spinning. If flicked correctly, there is very little waste, just fluff and dirt remaining on the carder. This semi-worsted yarn has the fibres in the parallel arrangement in which they grew, but the short fibres still remain.

6 This is the one I call 'almost worsted'. The

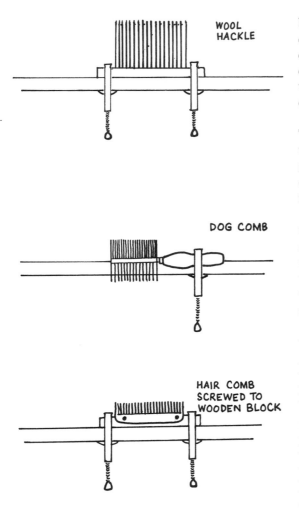

46. Wool combing tools firmly attached to a table

First I sorted and washed my Teeswater fleece, being careful not to agitate the wool so that the crimpy locks stayed intact and did not felt. After drying, I sprayed the fleece lightly with an oil emulsion (1 pint of water to $\frac{1}{4}$ pint of oil, plus 1 teaspoonful of ammonia) and left it rolled up for a day before using.

Some textile supply shops stock wool hackles. They comprise a hardwood base with two rows of teeth set in, and usually come with a clamp. A good substitute for the wool hackle is a metal dog comb or a strong hair comb. Some way must be found to clamp the comb to a table (see fig. 46).

Take one lock of wool at a time and carefully tease it. My Teeswater fleece was reasonably open at the shorn end, but the curly tips needed patient teasing to avoid breaking them in the comb. Hold the teased lock firmly by the shorn end and flick the tips over the teeth, and pull through the comb.

Flick only the tips over at first, then work your way up the staple with each successive combing. Attempting to pull nearly all the staple through the teeth on the first combing may result in knotted or broken fibres and too much waste. When you have combed more than half the staple, turn the lock around and repeat the process, holding the tips. As each lock is combed, take out the noils which remain, otherwise they will build up and clog the comb. Place the combed locks by you, with all the tips in the same direction. Then you can spin from each individual lock, or tie several locks loosely together, or make a roving.

To make a roving, the locks must be placed in a line, overlapping each other by about half their length, with the tips in the same direction. Start at one end and, with your hands only a few inches apart, stretch the fibres out a few inches. Work along the length of overlapped locks, trying to keep constant the distance you pull apart. If you pull too far apart then thin or broken parts will develop and these will have to be relapped. To make a uniform roving requires a little practice. The attenuated fibres hold together better if a small amount of twist is applied. Roll the roving

fibres are hackled or combed through a wool hackle, dog comb or strong hair comb. The fibres are parallel in the yarn and most of the short noils are removed. However, it doesn't remove the short fibres as thoroughly as woollen combs do, nor does it mix the fibres properly. The combed locks are also more difficult to draw into a roving. But it is a quick method and does produce a reasonably smooth, shiny and strong yarn with little effort. I recommend it and it's the one I describe for making the warp yarn.

between your hands and then it can be coiled and placed on your lap ready for spinning.

I spun my plied warp yarns with a 10.5:1 wheel ratio using a worsted draw. The scales on a wool fibre grow from the root downwards, so you will get a smoother yarn if you spin from the shorn ends of the staples: the scaly fibres will be smoothed by the front hand as it glides over the yarn.

On a long stapled wool, the draw between the hands will be long – about the length of the staple. As this is a warp yarn it must be fine enough to go through the holes and slits in the heddle, and have enough twist to make a smooth, abrasion-resistant yarn. A hairy or delicate warp yarn may need to be strengthened with a warp dressing, such as gelatine, but a well spun 'almost worsted' yarn should be in no danger of breaking or becoming too 'sticky' (a term used to describe fuzzy warp yarns which adhere to each other and form an imperfect shed).

The weft yarns I spun with a worsted draw using a 6.5:1 wheel ratio. The wool was teased and carded and the webs rolled across the cards. The short fibres were included, making it a soft, semi-worsted singles yarn.

The following working outline is for a 34 to 36 inch (86 to 91 cm) jacket. For a larger size, four widths instead of three will be needed in the lower half, so allow an extra 15 inches (38 cm) to be added to the first length of fabric. If you want longer sleeves, add a few more inches on to the length of the second fabric.

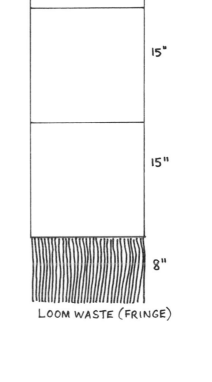

LOOM WASTE (FRINGE)

8"
20 cm

15"
38 cm

15"

15"

8"

LOOM WASTE (FRINGE)

47.

FABRIC FOR LOWER HALF OF JACKET

Rigid heddle $15\frac{3}{4}$ inches (40 cm) long, with 10 spaces per inch. The warp was spaced, which gave a vertical stripe effect in the finished cloth. Find the centre of the heddle and work out the spacing, leaving a hole and space at each end, and thread (see fig. 48). The length of fabric is made up as in fig. 47.

HEDDLE CENTRE

| MIDDLE 5 | 17 ENDS | 5 SPACE | 17 ENDS | 5 SPACE | 17 ENDS | 5 SPACE | 15 ENDS (3 DOUBLE) |

48. Warp spaced fabric divided to make jacket body

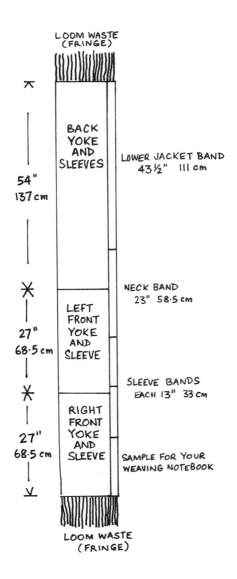

LOOM WASTE
(FRINGE)

⊼

BACK
YOKE
AND
SLEEVES

LOWER JACKET BAND
43½" 111 cm

54"
137 cm

✳

LEFT
FRONT
YOKE
AND
SLEEVE

NECK BAND
23" 58.5 cm

27"
68.5 cm

✳

SLEEVE BANDS
EACH 13" 33 cm

RIGHT
FRONT
YOKE
AND
SLEEVE

27"
68.5 cm

SAMPLE FOR YOUR
WEAVING NOTEBOOK

⋁

LOOM WASTE
(FRINGE)

49.

FABRIC FOR YOKE, SLEEVES AND BANDS

For each selvedge allow three extra ends, making a total of 155 warp ends. These are threaded through the heddle to give a balanced weave. The cloth is made up as in fig. 49.

The measurements for this second length of fabric allow for a shrinkage rate about ¾ inch for every 12 inches (2 cm every 30.5 cm). My fabric did not shrink quite as much as this, but it is wise to allow it nevertheless.

After removing fabric from the loom, any loose ends should be sewn back in prior to washing. This wash is a gentle process to relax the fibres, not a finishing process as with a woollen yarn cloth. Hang the fabric on a line to drip dry and then press it on the wrong side while it is still damp.

The fabric is cut out to the measurements in fig. 50, allowing extra for seams. The jacket is stitched by machine, using open seams, neatened by zig-zagging over the raw edges. Small bands of ¾ inch (2 cm) at the neck, cuffs and lower edge give a neat and professional finish. These are machine-sewn, right sides together, then folded over and slip stitched into place by hand. For the fringes, the cut off waste yarn is equally divided between the back and front yoke and included in the seam, so a second line of stitching will be needed to secure it. Finally, I lined my jacket with matching material.

5. Shading technique demands careful blending of natural colours during carding and spinning.

6. A variety of shades – as in this cardigan – can be obtained easily by dyeing with onion skins.

7. Natural, undyed wool from many different breeds produced this 'coat of many colours'.

8. Cardigans combining thick singles and fine plied yarns – one from Jacob fleece, the other from a Suffolk fleece dyed with elderberries.

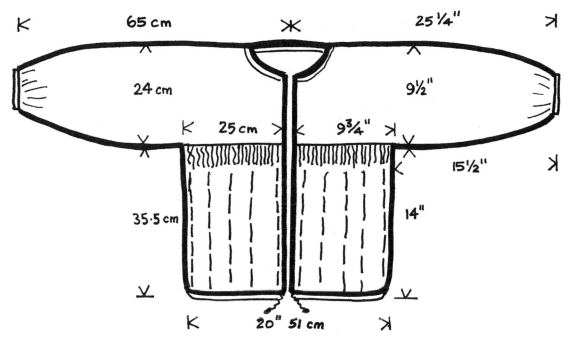

65 cm · 25¼"

24 cm · 9½"

25 cm · 9¾"

15½"

35·5 cm · 14"

20" 51 cm

50.

13 Chunky one-piece jacket

This jacket is knitted in a single piece on large wooden needles. It can be reversible if you like (so don't sew in a label and make the underarm seam neat). It's quick and easy to make, yet the simple lines really show off a beautiful handspun yarn to best advantage. Finishing the edges with a silky home-made bias binding gives the jacket a 'dressy' look, so it teams well with skirts and trousers.

The Jacob fleece I chose to use was 90 per cent dark brown, with an average staple length of $3\frac{1}{2}$ inches (9 cm). It came from an older sheep and was quite hairy, though not kempy. But when spun and washed it made a lovely soft, lofty yarn in subtle shades of brown.

The fleece was sorted and skirted, removing a small white patch. On closer inspection, the colour seemed to darken towards the britch end, so I separated this section for blending later. This fleece was only a few days old and exceptionally clean so I broke the rules and spun it in the grease. Normally, when spinning a very thick yarn, the wool should be washed first otherwise dirt becomes irretrievably trapped.

A thick yarn can be spun on a jumbo flyer, but I decided to use my Indian spinner. This has a very low ratio of 2.9:1 – ideal for the job. Bulky yarns need little twist and a wheel with a good draw-in rate, which a bobbin driven wheel provides.

I spun all the fleece the same day. Wool from the darker of the two piles was blended in and I carded a dozen rolags at a time. These were gobbled up by the wheel in minutes. As the fleece was hairy and long stapled, I spun with a worsted draw, smoothing stray hairs back into the yarn with my front hand. I prefer to use this worsted short draw for a bulky yarn: there are so many fibres to control that it's the best way of producing a smoother, less hairy yarn. One thick yarn, even if plied, has relatively little twist so that fibres sticking out from a woollen spun bulky yarn would soon work loose. This is what causes garments to become badly pilled.

Instructions for use of the Indian spinner advise against overfilling the bobbin, and it became heavy to treadle when more than three-quarters full – hardly surprising as the bobbin holds 34 oz (965 g)! I had only the one large bobbin, so in order to ply the yarn I had to wind off each half-full bobbin and place the balls in empty boxes to prevent them rolling about. After plying and hanking (with a wide-armed niddy-noddy) the yarn was soaked for an hour in warm water and then left overnight in a detergent solution. When rinsed and dry, it was wound into balls. Each giant ball was bigger than a football, wonderfully soft and bouncy, and three were used for the jacket. A remaining half-size ball was made into a bag (see next project). These Indian spinning wheels are not too popular in England at the time of writing, but certainly I enjoy using mine.

51. A single Jacob fleece weighing 2 lb 4 oz (1050 g)
was used to make this knitted jacket and its matching bag

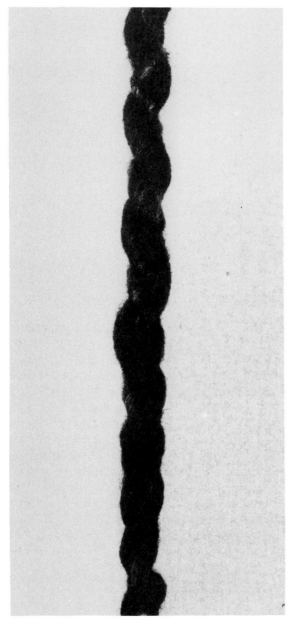

52.

Jumbo flyer attachments normally have a low wheel ratio (the Ashford jumbo is 4.3:1) and if you treadle slowly it is possible to make a thick, loosely twisted yarn.

Here is the method I use for making a basic knitting pattern for handspun yarn: choose what seems to be the right needle size and knit a small square of about 5 inches (13 cm). Does the knitted fabric feel right? If it's hard and solid, use a bigger needle; if it's too loose and open, use a smaller one. I have seen many handspinners spoil their work by knitting on needles too small and producing a very stiff fabric. Handspun yarns, because they are not subjected to harsh commercial processes, are as soft and springy as the natural wool itself, so they must be knitted in a way that preserves these qualities. Once you're happy with the test square, press it and count the stitches. For example, in this project I had 3 stitches to 2 inches, so the calculation for a 38 inch hip, allowing 2 inches for ease of wearing, was easy: 60 stitches will give the required 40 inches. I avoid side seams if possible and start by knitting the back and front together. Having knitted the body of the garment to the correct size it is quite easy to measure the length of sleeve you need and calculate the number of stitches. If in doubt when working out a sleeve pattern, always choose a smaller number of stiches because knitted sleeves tend to stretch lengthways.

For this jacket I used the largest knitting needles I could find and even then made each stitch slightly bigger than the needle by giving the stitch a slight pull before knitting the next one. Clip-type clothes pegs proved useful for preventing the stitches from slipping off the ends of the needles. Because the garment is knitted in one piece, the knitting becomes heavy to work with towards the end, but this disadvantage is outweighed by the lack of seams.

PATTERN FOR JACKET

Size: 36 inches (91 cm)
Equipment: 2 pairs size 000 wooden needles, the longest you can buy. 6 clip-type clothes pegs.
Tension: 3 sts to 2 inches.
Cast on 60 sts.
Work in st st until work measures $13\frac{1}{2}$ inches (34 cm) or length required.
Divide and mark work as follows: right front 15 sts, back 30 sts, left front 15 sts.

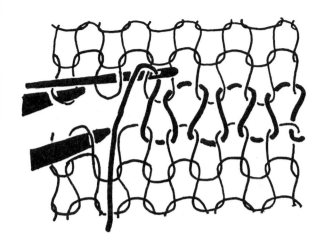

53. Grafting together two pieces of stocking stitch fabric

Work on rt front: K 15 sts, cast on 17 sts.

Continue in st st on these 32 sts until work measures 4 inches (10 cm) from armhole.

Shape neck: cast off 3 sts, work to end of row.

Work 3 more rows dec 1 st at neck edge on each row.

Leave remaining 26 sts on a spare needle with pegs at each end and leave about 36 inches (91 cm) of yarn (to graft seam) before breaking off.

Rejoin yarn to 15 sts of left front and repeat neck shaping and sleeves as for right front.

Join yarn to 30 sts of back.

K 30, cast on 17, turn.

P 47 sts, cast on 17.

Continue in st st on these 64 st until work measures 7½ inches (19 cm) from armhole. Break off yarn.

Graft right back to right front at shoulders and sleeve (26 sts × 2) as shown in fig. 53.

Rejoin yarn to middle 12 sts and cast off these for neck.

Graft remaining 52 sts of left shoulder and sleeve.

Sew underarm seams neatly.

To graft, thread the matching yarn through a large bodkin or similar. Place the two pieces to be grafted right side (smooth side) uppermost with the needles parallel. Take off one stitch at a time from alternate needles and sew as in fig. 53.

A good quality and matching lining material provided me with 130 inches (331 cm) of homemade bias binding. It was easier to sew on by hand as my sewing machine did not cope well with such thick material. The binding was sewn on right sides together using a backstitch and stretching the bias slightly. Fold the binding over the raw edges and slip stitch into place – very neatly if you want a reversible jacket. The neck tie was one strip 55 inches (140 cm) long with the two tie ends slip stitched together.

14 Knitted shoulder bag

A knitted bag is more unusual than the popular woven type, especially when worn with a matching jacket. This knitted shoulder bag was made with left-over yarn from the jacket described in the previous project. The theme of the jacket was carried through in the design of the bag by using covered piping.

7 oz (198 g) of thickly spun wool is knitted into a rectangle 11 by 23 inches (28 by 58.5 cm) on large wooden needles size 000 with 16 stitches. Pin out the finished knitting and press to shape. Cut out some strong lining material (as used for the jacket bias binding) just over 1 inch (3 cm)

wider and longer than the knitting. Pin the lining centrally to the knitting with the wrong sides together and then tack into position. Fold, and press down $\frac{1}{8}$ inch (3 mm) hem, to the wrong side, on both long edges of the lining as shown in fig. 54. You need some piping cord a quarter inch thick (about 1 cm) in two lengths of 23 inches (58.5 cm) and one of 41 inches (104 cm). Lay one of the shorter lengths of cord down one of the long sides of the bag with the right side of the knitting uppermost: it should just fit. Fold over the hemmed lining material (see fig. 55). Slip stitch the lining into place close to the knitted

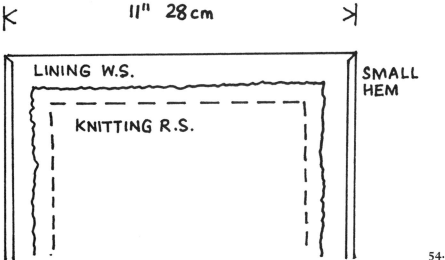

11" 28 cm

LINING W.S.

KNITTING R.S.

SMALL HEM

54.

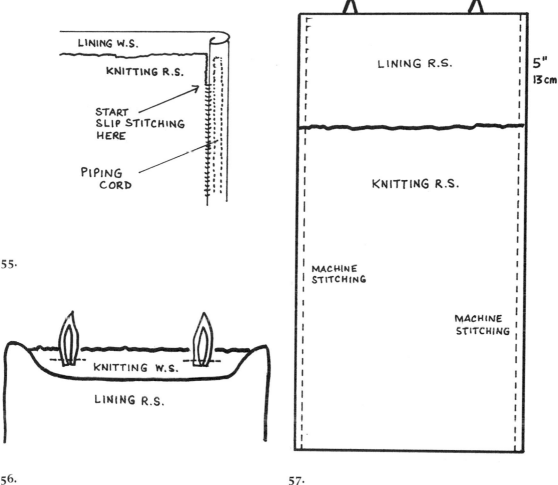

55.

56.

57.

edge, starting and finishing about 2 inches (5 cm) from the top and bottom. Do exactly the same at the other long edge.

Cut a piece of lining material 7 by 1¾ inches (18 by 4.5 cm) for the loops. With the right sides together sew at the edge of the material. Turn right side out. Cut the strip into two. Sew these two loops into position at the inside top edge of the bag, as shown in fig. 56.

Fold over the 1 inch (2.5 cm) of lining to the inside at the top and bottom of the knitting and slip stitch into position. Fold the corners over the

piping as neatly as you can and slip stitch the remaining 2 inches (5 cm). Now fold the rectangle to make a bag, having 5 inches (13 cm) at the top to fold over and pin into position. Machine stitch in the groove between the piping and the knitting (the stitches will not show). Go over this stitching again to strengthen the seam (fig. 57).

Cut out a piece of lining material the length of the remaining piece of piping cord and about 1¾ inches (4.5 cm) wide. This material will fit more smoothly over the cord if you cut it out on the bias fold. Fold the lining strip right sides together and stitch near the raw edge, leaving enough width for the cord to fit through. Turn the strip right side out and thread the piping cord through. The easiest way to do this is to sew a strong thread (button cotton) to the end of the cord, stitching through all three or four main threads, and take the needle through the lining tube. Then slowly pull the cord through.

Push the covered cord through the knitting at the back of the bag and sew firmly into position. My stitches didn't show through the bulky yarn. Cover two buttons with the lining material and sew in position under the loops. Wood or horn buttons would look good too.

15 Navajo Indian style rug

I first discovered the Navajo loom when searching for some inexpensive looms for a handspinning class. What an exciting discovery it was too, for although primitive, it is truly ingenious. Here is a loom which can be made easily at little or no cost, is portable, and yet can withstand the extreme warp tension needed for rugmaking. It's excellent for other projects too, such as tapestries, gauze weaves, fleece and pile rugs, hangings – in fact anything where the rapid changing of sheds is not essential. It's much better than a back strap loom for weaving wide fabric. Being vertical, the Navajo loom is ideal for tapestries or any complex weft-faced design because the weaver can stand back and view the work from a distance.

The Navajo Indians of the south west states of America have been weaving on vertical looms for hundreds of years. It is the women of the tribe who weave. Some historians believe they may have been influenced by their neighbours, the Pueblo Indians. It was the Pueblo men who wove and they used cotton, whereas the Navajo, with their flocks of sheep, always wove with wool and sometimes goat hair.

The weaver sat in front of the loom on a skin, and as the work progressed she made the pile of skins higher. To make the loom stable, the Navajo often improvised by using two adjacent trees for the outer frame, or they secured it to the hogan (house). For a big rug, if there weren't any convenient trees, two large uprights were set into the ground and made firm by piling rocks around them. The Navajo were a semi-nomadic tribe, so the loom structure was only temporary. The inner loom could be dismantled and rolled up at any moment, even with the weaving in progress.

The Navajo wove four-selvedge blankets on their looms, initially for clothing and tent insulation, and then as rugs, which became their main item of trade. Having four strong selvedges on a rug increases its durability: only two selvedges are woven on a treadle floor loom. The early rugs were striped with natural fleece colours, but then the Navajo developed their distinctive style and wove colourful and intricate designs.

The loom I made is large and heavy enough to enable me to weave with it propped against a wall. Some of my students have made looms half the size, but because they were so light the main frame tended to twist and so had to be fixed to something permanent. If you don't want to fix your loom, I suggest you make it at least the size of mine. Whatever size the woven project is, the outer frame must be at least 1 foot (30 cm) bigger all round. To make a Navajo loom for a four selvedge rug measuring 22 by 34 inches (56 by 86 cm), this is what you will need:

WARPING FRAME

This makeshift structure is used only in the warping process.

58. Partly completed rug on Navajo loom

2 pieces scrap wood $45 \times 2\frac{1}{2} \times 2$ inches ($114 \times 6.5 \times 5$ cm).

2 pieces scrap wood $28 \times 2\frac{1}{2} \times 2$ inches ($71 \times 6.5 \times 5$ cm).

8 two-inch (5 cm) nails.

4 three-inch (7.5 cm) nails.

OUTER LOOM FRAME

This rectangular frame is made from four stout, straight tree branches lashed together to make a firm, rigid support for the inner loom.

2 branches $1\frac{1}{2}$ to $2\frac{1}{2}$ inches (4 to 6 cm) thick and 52 inches (132 cm) long.

2 branches $1\frac{1}{2}$ to $2\frac{1}{2}$ inches (4 to 6 cm) thick and $39\frac{1}{2}$ inches (100 cm) long.

23 yards (21 m) of clothes line or rope.

INNER LOOM AND WEAVING EQUIPMENT

I cheated and used three pieces of dowelling, but you can use smooth, straight sticks of similar dimensions.

3 pieces of dowelling, or broom handles, or sticks $\frac{3}{4}$ to $\frac{7}{8}$ inch (2 cm) thick and 30 inches (76 cm) long.

1 ball strong twine.

1 piece of dowelling $\frac{1}{4}$ inch (1 cm) thick and 29 inches (74 cm) long for the heddle rod.

1 smooth flat stick 26 inches (66 cm) long and $1\frac{3}{4}$ inches (3 cm) wide for the shed stick.

2 flat sticks for battens, one $\frac{3}{4}$-inch (2 cm) wide and 25 inches (63 cm) long, $\frac{1}{4}$ inch (0.5 cm) thick, the other $\frac{1}{2}$ inch (1.25 cm) wide and 25 inches (63 cm) long, $\frac{3}{8}$ inch (1 cm) thick.

1 kitchen fork.

1 large wool needle or mattress needle.

2 thin smooth sticks 27 inches (69 cm) long for the cross sticks.

PREPARING THE WARP YARN

The warp yarn takes a lot of strain so it must be very strong. I used 5 oz (140 g) of Yak hair, but any long stapled wool or hair may be used. Yak hair is from the outer coat of this ox-like animal,

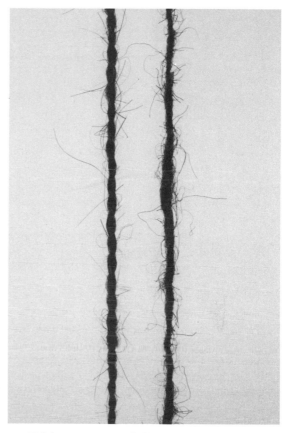

59. Yak hair warp yarn (left). Herdwick weft yarn (right)

found chiefly in Tibet. The Yak hair was black, wiry and slippery and the fibres about 6 inches (15 cm) long. My tops were bought from a mill that manufactured coat interlining. I spun the yarn using a worsted short draw method. It needed practice to achieve a yarn with sufficient twist and at the same time prevent the twist running into the undrafted fibres. I found it easier to put the driving band on my larger flyer groove (wheel ratio 6.5:1) and fill a bobbin, then respin, letting the yarn glide at an even rate through my fingers. This produced a hard, twisted and slightly bristly yarn which needed care when plying to avoid snarls. If slightly undertwisted the slippery fibres tend to drift apart, causing the yarn to break.

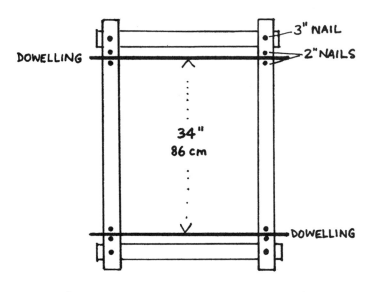

60. Warping frame

The Navajo spun their yarns on large spindles, which they rolled on the thigh (a method described elsewhere in this book). They often respun their warp yarns two or three times to get the necessary twist. Wind the plied warp yarn into a ball.

MAKING THE WARPING FRAME

Assemble the warping frame as in fig. 60 using the 3-inch nails to join the pieces of wood. Two lengths of dowelling ($\frac{7}{8}$ inch, (2 cm), thick) which you set aside for the inner loom are placed on the longer lengths of wood 34 inches (86 cm) apart. Hammer in the 2 inch nails each side of the dowelling to hold in position. The frame should be high enough from the floor to allow the ball of warp yarn to pass underneath the dowelling.

WARPING THE LOOM

I warped my loom at 6 ends per inch (about 12 ends per 5 cm). Mark the width of the rug on the doweiling (22 inches/56 cm) then divide and mark off into quarters. Each quarter has 33 warp ends (total warp ends: 6 × 22 = 132, divide by 4 = 33). Tie the warp yarn to one of the lengths of dowelling and take it across to the other, over this, back to the first, taking it over this and thus forming a figure of eight with the yarn (fig. 61). This makes *two* warp ends. Continue, keeping the tension reasonably tight and even and avoiding the tendency to warp tighter and tighter as you go along. When all 132 ends have been warped tie the yarn to a length of dowelling, keeping the tension, and cut off the remainder.

To preserve the cross, place the cross sticks in the space at each end of the warp and slide them to the middle. Tie the sticks together at each end. Check that the warp is spaced evenly on both lengths of dowelling.

TWINING THE WARP

To space the warp permanently and to strengthen the top and bottom selvedges, some cord is twined around the warp ends. The twining cord – remaining warp yarn is ideal – is cut to about five times the width of the warp and doubled. An overhand knot is tied 3 inches (7.5 cm) from the loop. Begin by encircling the twining cord round the first warp end on one piece of dowelling. As

61. The warp must form a figure-of-eight between the two pieces of dowelling

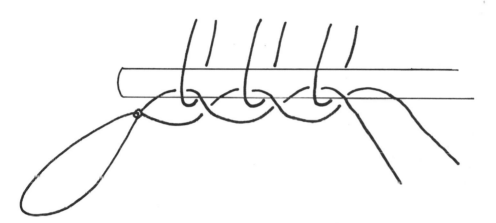

62. Spacing the warp by twining

shown in fig. 62, twist the cords then encircle the second warp thread. Usually, one twist between each warp is enough, but if there is a wide gap two and sometimes three twists might be needed to fill the space between each warp. Repeat the twining until the last warp thread is reached, then tie the cord in an overhand knot leaving 3 inches (7.5 cm) before cutting off. Repeat this twining on the other piece of dowelling.

BINDING THE WARP

The next step is to bind the warp on to lengths of dowelling. It is this ingenious technique which enables the rug to be woven with a bound selvedge on all four sides. Take the third piece of $\frac{7}{8}$ inch (2 cm) dowelling and place it adjacent to the bottom length of dowelling on the warping frame. Thread a large needle with twine and tie the end to the new piece of dowelling. Take the twine between the warp threads and around the new dowelling as shown in fig. 63, thus sewing the twining to the second length of dowelling.

The twine must go cleanly between the dowelling and the twining; take care not to catch the threads with the needle. When the length of twine runs out, just knot on a new piece, as this twine will later be cut from the finished rug. When the binding is finished, take out the first piece of dowelling – this can now be laid adjacent to the top dowelling and the binding repeated at this end. When completed, take out the inner dowelling as before and remove the warp, end dowellings and cross sticks from the warping frame.

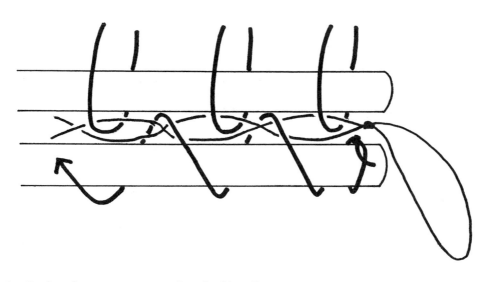

63. Binding the warp on to a new length of dowelling

MAKING THE OUTER LOOM FRAME

Make the outer loom frame by lashing together the branches. Mine stayed rigid for many weeks, though eventually I had to put a nail through one join – a very un-Indian practice.

FITTING THE WARP INTO THE MAIN FRAME

To set the warp into the frame, place the loom frame upright with the warp stretched out on the floor in front of it. Tie the bottom warp dowelling (which should now be called the cloth beam) to the lower branch of the frame at each end and in the middle. Use doubled twine for this and make the ties so that there is about 2 inches (5 cm) between the cloth beam and loom frame, checking that the beam lies horizontal. You may have to vary the lengths of the ties to compensate for any unevenness in the loom frame. Make three similar ties to the top dowelling of the warp (which we will now call the warp beam) and the third piece of $\frac{7}{8}$ inch (2 cm) dowelling.

The next stage is to bind the third piece of dowelling to the top of the loom frame in such a way as to be able to regulate the warp tension. Using the remaining rope or line fasten it to the

far end of the top branch of the frame. Now loop it over the dowelling and back over the loom frame, keeping the tension tight. Repeat this about six times evenly along the length of dowelling and loom frame. Finishing by warping the end loosely around the frame twice then push the rope under these loops before pulling tight. The tension should be tight. If it is not, you can adjust it by pulling on the rope along the slack part until you get an even tension.

MAKING THE SHEDS

The final task is to make the heddles and insert the shed stick so that the two sheds can be made easily. The top shed is simple. Undo the ties securing the cross sticks. Take the shed stick – that's the flat piece of wood $1\frac{1}{4}$ inches (3 cm) wide – and place it in the space occupied by the top cross stick. Remove the cross stick. I made a hole at each end of my shed stick so I could thread string through and fasten it to the warp beam above, an advisable precaution if you intend moving your loom about a lot.

To make the heddles, take the end of the ball of twine or softer string if you have some and carry

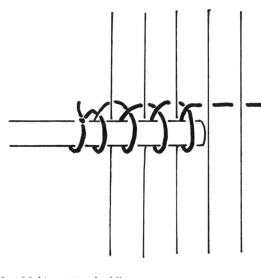

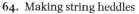

64. Making string heddles

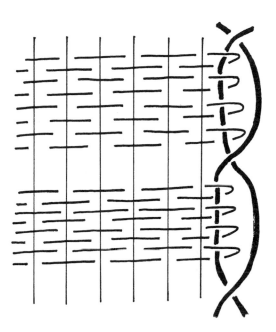

65. A whipped selvedge

the end from right to left through the space made by the second cross stick. Attach the end of the string loosely to the right-hand side of the heddle rod (the $\frac{1}{4}$ inch/1 cm dowelling) held at the left of the loom. Starting at the left of the warp, pull up the string with the right index finger from between the first two front warp ends. Pull the string into a loop, twist it and slip it onto the heddle rod as in fig. 64.

The length of string between the warp and the heddle rod should be about $1\frac{1}{4}$ inches (3 cm). Continue making these heddles to the end of the warp, pushing the heddles down the rod as you go. To ensure an even shed, make the heddles as even as possible: they can be adjusted, but it's simpler to start with them all the same length.

SELVEDGE CORDS

The side selvedges of a rug must be strengthened. This is usually achieved by doubling the last few warp ends at each side or setting the warp closer at the edges. The Navajo technique is known as a whipped or bound edge, which gives a neatly twined selvedge similar to that made on the top and bottom of the warp.

Take some of the remaining warp yarn – about five times the length of the warp – then twist and fold it back on itself, making a four-ply cord. Double the cord and loop the folded end over the cloth beam at one side of the warp and tie. The other ends are tied loosely to the warp beam. Repeat this for the other side. When weaving starts, the weft is wrapped around one half of the cord each time it is taken round the last warp end, as shown in fig. 65. When about eight threads have encircled the cord, it is twisted and the other half of the cord brought forward to receive the next eight weft threads. You may count your threads or measure the build-up of weft before twisting the cord, providing you devise a way of making equal gaps between the twists. After a while, twist builds up on the cord and you will have to release it by undoing the knot on the warp beam and then retying it.

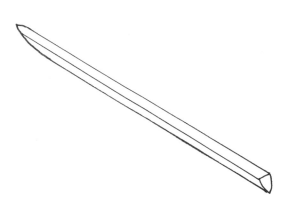

66. Batten shaped to glide easily through the warp.

WEAVING TOOLS

Before weaving it's worth spending a little time on your battens. They will slide through the sheds easier if you shape one end to a gentle curve and sandpaper the stick so that one long edge is nearly pointed (fig. 66). Some weavers use this sharp edge to beat down the weft, but I use a kitchen fork. The Navajo treasured their weaving tools, handing them down from one generation to the next. The batten must be smooth so it doesn't catch on the warp.

WEAVING THE RUG

Navajo rug design is a subject which could form an entire book, so here are just a few ideas. Probably the easiest traditional design to weave is that of horizontal stripes. It's a good way of using up odd bits of fleeces too. Although simple in design, it was these striped rugs which first drew attention to the Navajo's weaving skills, so perfectly were they made. Or you may choose a simple design incorporating square (fig. 67) or triangle shapes. Always start and finish the rug with about 2 inches (5 cm) of plain coloured weave. This makes it easier to weave the top section.

The Navajo wove with many natural coloured fleeces, often adding just one dyed yarn. They wove from memory, only using cartoons if weaving to commission or copying another rug. Often, the original design was adapted or altered as the weaving progressed. If you start with a simple plan as in fig. 67 and all goes well, you can add more shapes in a plain area.

Where colours met, there were two ways in which the Navajo joined them: the interlock technique and the turned weft technique. Sometimes both were used in the same rug. The interlocked weft produces a sharp colour join, whereas the turned lock produces a slightly serrated join and a small build-up of weft. The latter was always considered the stronger join until recently when some rug restorers thought the build up of weft strained the warp thread and actually helped to weaken it. I used the interlocked technique for my rug.

All tapestry techniques can be used on a Navajo loom, so if you want to weave a complicated design and are unfamiliar with the procedure, refer to a weaving book (see bibliography).

For my weft I used coarse wool: a Herdwick hog fleece, some Black Welsh and some white Welsh dyed yellow with young bracken shoots. It was spun with a little more twist than a normal singles yarn, so was washed then dried under tension. It should be thick enough to pack down and cover the warp completely, making a very firm, weft-faced fabric. The weft is wound into finger hanks except when working one colour from selvedge to selvedge, when a small stick shuttle can be used. The Navajo way is to use a small stick with a notch cut in one end to hold the weft.

To start weaving, the pairs of warp ends must be broken up. Place the first four rows in, top and bottom of the warp, with the fingers. Take the weft over two, then under two, continuing to the end of the warp, then back again, placing the weft under where it went over in the previous row, and over where it went under. Make two more

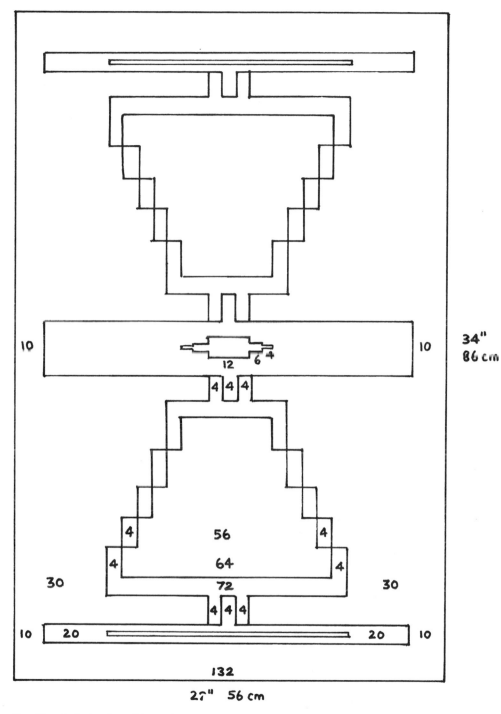

67. Simple design for a 'Navajo' rug. Figures in the
diagram refer to the number of warp ends

journeys and then repeat these four rows at the top, pushing the weft up instead of beating it down.

Now you're ready to use the proper sheds. The top shed, or stick shed, is made by bringing down the shed stick to just above the heddles and turning the stick on its side. Put the larger batten in the space formed below the heddle rod. Flatten the shed stick and return it to the top of the warp. Turn the batten on edge, making a good shed. The batten should stay in this position if the warp is tight enough, if not tighten the top rope. Put your weft through this shed and around one half of the edge twining cord. The next shed is made by pulling in the middle of the heddle rod, which brings the back threads forwards. Guide the batten through this shed and turn on end, as before.

When nearing the top of the rug the weaving becomes more difficult and the smaller batten must be used. The shed stick cannot be turned on end, but will simply be pushed towards the heddles. As the shed becomes narrower the shed stick is replaced with a thin wire (a straightened metal coat hanger is ideal) and finally the heddles and stick will have to be removed together with the shed rod. At this stage you will have to rely on picking up the warp ends a few at a time and then inserting the wire. The weft is put in with a large wool needle, sacking needle or umbrella rib and is pushed down. Then another weft can be put in above the wire and pushed up to the top of the rug. The final rows of weft will have to be darned in. Make sure the end of the rug is as tightly woven as the beginning. Darn in until you think no more weft can be put in – and then force in four more rows! You may find that your short lengths of handspun become a little untwisted as they are being pushed through such tight sheds, so give each length a few twists before you insert it. As you weave upwards, do not try to include the edge twining.

When you have finished, undo the top rope, then the three ties at the top and bottom. Untie the selvedge cords from the dowelling then pull out the binding twine at the top and bottom, taking care not to damage the twining. Thread the top of the edge twining cord through a needle and weave in the last few inches in the same way as you did the rest of the side selvedge. Tie the four ends of twining cord together in an over-hand knot at each corner.

I have had plenty of fun weaving on a Navajo loom and continue to admire the ingenuity, skill and artistry of those Indian weavers. Try it and you'll see what I mean: you will not be disappointed.

16 Loop yarn fabric

There are various ways of making handspun textured or fancy yarns. Some of these yarns look beautiful in themselves, but then quite ordinary or sometimes even peculiar when knitted. Many textured yarns show better in woven rather than knitted fabric. However, here is a loop yarn I spin which doesn't take much longer to make than an ordinary plied yarn and is equally effective woven or knitted. Crocheting with this yarn is more difficult, because the loops obscure the stitches to be worked.

A loop yarn can be made by two methods. The first involves using two handspun singles Z spun (clockwise) which are then plied with an S twist (anti-clockwise). One thread must be fine and tightly spun and this may be cotton, worsted spun wool, mohair or silk. The other thread must be thicker and softly spun. My favourites are mohair, dog hair or a lustre wool.

A fine silk singles and a thicker mohair singles is the combination I chose. The silk was Z spun from Tussah silk tops into a fine, tightly twisted yarn using a worsted draw with a 10.5:1 wheel ratio. The mohair was Z spun from tops using a worsted draw and a 6.5:1 wheel ratio to give a thicker, loosely spun yarn.

The two yarns are plied (S twist) by holding the silk tighter than the mohair, so that the mohair hair coils itself round the silk. If you're plying from a lazy kate on the floor it helps if the mohair bobbin is above the silk one. After a few inches

have been plied, stop the wheel and push up the mohair into loops with the thumb and index finger of the right hand, as shown in fig. 70. A light flick rather than a strong push is needed. A quick flick will produce a large loop, whereas a slower flick will result in a series of smaller loops. Once you can see how the yarn is forming, it should be possible to continue treadling as you make the loops.

You will soon realise why the silk must be tightly spun. In theory it needs just the extra twist enabling you to hold it long enough for the mohair to loop, because as you are holding it the silk is untwisting. With practice you should be able to make a balanced yarn suitable for knitting or for use as a weft, without setting the twist. If at first the loop yarn twists back on itself when in hank form, soak it in warm water for a few minutes and then hang it to dry with a weight attached.

A second method for making a loop yarn involves the use of ordinary commercial sewing machine cotton and one handspun singles thread. A thread of sewing cotton – the core of the yarn – and a Z spun singles are plied with an S twist, the handspun yarn forming the loops. Another sewing cotton thread, called the binder, is then plied with the loop yarn in a Z twist, so making a balanced yarn and securing the loops.

I think it's worth experimenting with different handspun singles for this yarn – now is your

68.

chance to make use of those small odd balls of handspun you have stored away. All hairy, shiny fibres work well, as do mixture yarns. For example, I found that a white Orlon and rabbit hair blend spun into a soft fine singles looked beautiful when looped around some coloured cotton.

Masham, a semi-lustre wool, also produces an exciting yarn when looped with cotton. The fleece is first washed and carded, with the webs rolled across the carder. It is softly spun into a Z singles using a worsted draw on a 6.5:1 wheel ratio. Hold the sewing thread tightly and push up the wool loops as you ply S twist. This will result in an unbalanced, kinky yarn. With a Z twist, now ply the loop yarn and a second length of sewing cotton. This gives a balanced yarn and if

necessary you can respace some of the loops before they are locked into position.

Large loops of thicker yarn may catch on the small cup hooks of the flyer. The following loops build up and form an ugly snarl. Use a jumbo flyer or replace the cup hooks with L-shaped ones. But remember to space these hooks evenly along the flyer: if they are all on one arm, it will be unbalanced. Another solution is to straighten some of the cup hooks with a pair of pliers.

I wove fabric from the silk and mohair loop yarn, using a warp of plied mohair. The $4\frac{1}{2}$ oz (128 g) of mohair warp was spun from tops using a worsted draw on a 10.5:1 wheel ratio. The fabric was woven on a 24-inch (61 cm) four-shaft table loom with a plain (tabby) weave. The warp

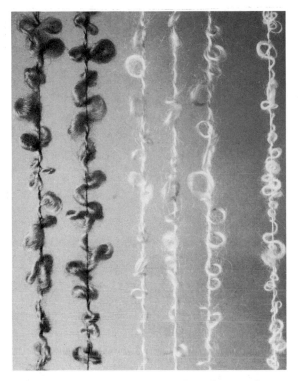

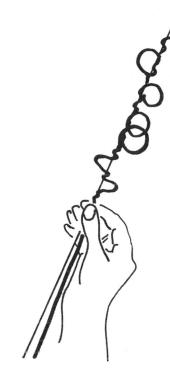

69. Loop yarns (from l. to r.): Masham fleece with sewing cotton, mohair and silk, rabbit hair and Orlon blend with sewing cotton

70. Making a loop yarn

was set at 6 ends per inch (12 ends per 5 cm) The length was 62 inches (158 cm) which allowed 18 inches (46 cm) for loom waste and 3 inches (7.5 cm) for shrinkage. Lightly beat each weft into place, leaving a little space between each pick, otherwise you'll end up with a rug! I used 9 picks to each inch (18 picks to 5 cm). After removing from the loom, secure the warp fringes and then wash well. Rinse, then remove excess water with a towel or spin dry before drying flat. The warp was $22\frac{1}{2}$ inches wide in the loom and after washing became 21 inches (53 cm). With this fabric, the silk yarn did not need pre-shrinking.

My intention was to weave some unusual cloth for a jacket, but no sooner had the fabric left the loom than it was seized by the family and has since been used as a knee rug and as a stole. This luxurious fabric will make a jacket . . . . one day.

17 Cotton summer top

When I began wearing clothes made from my early attempts at handspinning, the yarns were mostly uneven or lumpy. This suited the style of garment admirably and my pride grew as complimentary remarks were made. Then I met an experienced handspinner. He said: 'OK, but really you can't call yourself a handspinner until you make something from a perfectly even yarn.'

It was a challenge my damaged pride could not resist. I had heard that cotton was difficult to spin. Right! I decided to make my perfect yarn from cotton.

Cotton fibres vary in length from just under $\frac{1}{2}$ to 2 inches (1.5 to 5 cm) and in colour from white to cream and brown. Natural brown cotton is not produced commercially, so English handspinners seldom have the chance to handle any. Small quantities are grown in South and Central America, Mexico, India and China. Although prized for its colour, it is coarse and only about $\frac{1}{2}$ inch in length. Commercial cotton growers are wary of this coloured strain as cross-pollination can easily occur with the white crop.

Commercially grown cotton can be divided into three main groups. The first includes Sea Island, which is the finest, silkiest and longest fibre, followed by Pima, and Egyptian, which are also very long and lustrous. Very little Sea Island cotton is produced. In the second group is American Upland cotton, varying in length from a $\frac{1}{2}$ to $1\frac{1}{2}$ inches (1.5 to 4 cm), and this is the one

most commonly available to handspinners. The third group consists of 'Old World' types, and includes many of the shorter fibres.

Cotton fibres are attached to seeds and resemble hollow tubes. As the seed pod or boll ripens and opens, the fibres dry and the inner canal collapses, leaving a flat, twisted ribbon-like shape. When spinning, it is these convolutions which help to keep the fibres together, so making a cohesive yarn. The wax-like coating on each fibre also aids the spinner. Cotton is highly absorbent. The yarns and fabrics are stronger wet than dry. Shrinkage rate varies depending on how it is spun and woven, most shrinkage occuring with a loosely woven, highly twisted yarn.

The cotton I spun for this knitted top was American Upland, with a fibre length of barely half an inch. The fibres were de-seeded but very compacted because of the method used for this purpose prior to shipping, so they needed opening up. Traditionally this was done by bowing or beating with a stick to give a light, fluffy mass. I loosened the fibres by pulling them between my hands and then carding lightly. Cotton carders have fine teeth set closely together, but you can use wool carders if you brush very lightly, ensuring the fibres lie on top of the teeth and do not become embedded.

Spinning a medium or fine cotton yarn can be easy and relaxing. Use a woollen short draw, or

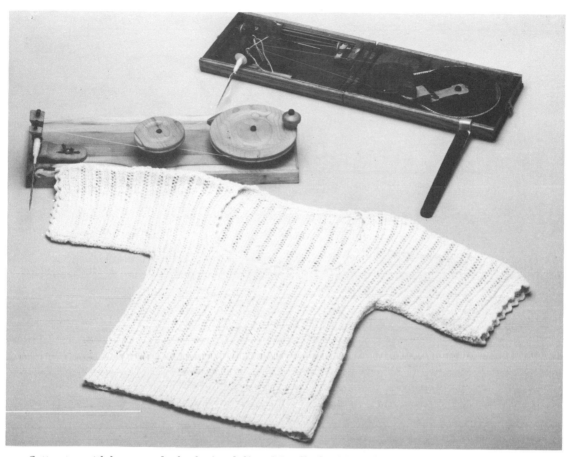

71. Cotton top with home-made charka (top left) and Gandhi 'book' charka (top right).

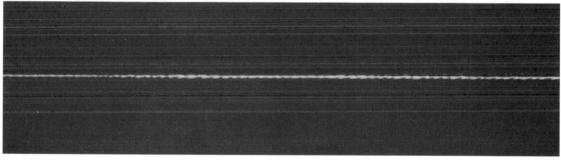

72.

long draw if you have carded the cotton. Worsted draw is a slow, tedious method of spinning short fibres and I would not recommend it for making a thin cotton yarn.

Cotton needs a high twist, especially if the yarn is to be fine. Use the highest wheel ratio you have, and even then it is likely that you will have to treadle quickly and draw back slowly. For a fine yarn, there should be the minimum of draw-in tension so slacken the brake or driving band on a

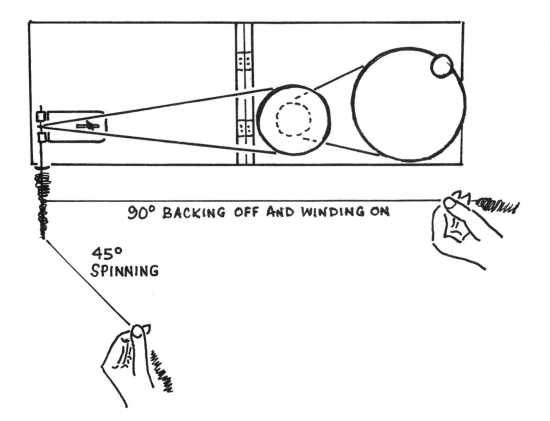

73. Spinning and winding on with Gandhi charka.

double band wheel. As you draw the rolag back, a very small drafting triangle is formed. At the end of the draw, check that the yarn is strong enough. If it isn't, treadle a few times before letting the yarn through the orifice. This applies particularly to the long draw.

My cotton fibres appeared to be white, but on spinning assumed an attractive cream colour. The colour of fibres always intensifies when they are spun. I plied my singles to make 7 oz (200 g) of balanced yarn. If you use a single thread, set the twist by first boiling it for a few minutes then hanging it up to dry with an appropriate weight attached.

To show off the yarn, I chose an open lacy stitch for the knitted top.

LACE PATTERN

Work off multiples of 6 plus 2.
Foundation row: K2 (P4, K2) to end.
Row 1: (right side) P2, (K2, Yf, sl1, K1, p.s.s.o., P2) to end.
Row 2: K2 (P2, y.r.n.P. 2tog K2)
These two rows form the pattern.

Many antique wheels have a high wheel ratio, small orifice and tiny hooks – ideal for spinning a fine cotton yarn. A simpler tool would be a lightweight spindle and this is how the famous Indian muslins were spun. So that the yarn does not have to support the weight of the spindle, the tip is rotated in a small bowl or shell. An improvement on the spindle for speed are the hand-turned spindle wheels.

Mahatma Gandhi, the political leader of India, said: 'For me nothing in the political world is more important than the spinning wheel.' He was determined to make a wheel which was inexpensive, portable, yet technically excellent for spinning cotton, so that all Indians could make their own clothes. Gandhi's charka as it is known, comes in two forms: an attaché case model and a book-size one. Both are very efficient.

The gearing is such that one turn of the wheel produces more than 60 turns of the spindle. Each model has its own hank winder which stows away neatly inside. My book-size charka is a delight to spin on. It never fails to intrigue students because of the ingenious way everything fits into such a tiny space, including two spare spindles. Because it is so small and light, a lever is

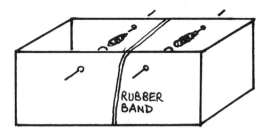

74. Small shoe box for improvised spindle lazy kate

supplied which fits over the side of the open 'book', so that the spinner can steady the charka with her foot.

The wheel is designed for use on the floor, the spinner sitting crosslegged alongside. To suit my Western bones, the charka goes on a table with a

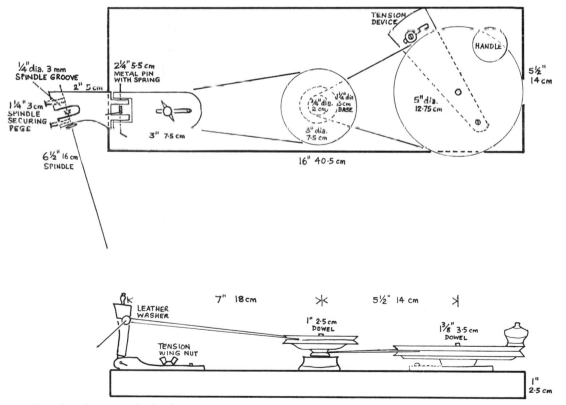

75. Plans for a home-made charka

weight on the lever and me on a chair. Rolags or punis are prepared. A puni is a tight thin rolag made by rolling a thin web of cotton firmly around a stick and then removing the stick.

Yarn is spun on a charka in a similar way to spinning on a Great Wheel. The right hand turns the wheel, whilst the left hand pulls back the rolag ahead of the twist at an angle of $45°$, drawing back to arms length. At the end of the draw the yarn is held whilst the wheel is turned a few times to give the necessary extra twist. It is wound on by first 'backing off' the yarn from the end of the spindle. The yarn is held at $90°$ to the spindle and the wheel reversed half a turn and then it is wound on the spindle in a cone shape as shown in fig. 73.

I asked a local woodturner to make me a charka style wheel in yew wood. It does not dismantle and fold away into a box and there is no hank winder, so I put my spindles in a shoe box and wind off on to a niddy-noddy (see fig. 74). The shoe box is also used for plying two fine yarns. I use both my charkas for spinning ultra-fine yarns of cotton and silk. There is no draw-in pull, as on a flyer wheel, making them ideal for spinning very finely. I have been unable to find anyone in the UK supplying Gandhi charkas, though they can be obtained in the United States. The home-made charka is a good alternative, if you possess the necessary skills to make one or can find someone who has: a plan is shown in fig.75.

18 Thick cotton parka

I made this hooded jacket from the same cotton – American Upland – as in the previous project. Although both garments started life the same colour, cream or ecru, the jacket is now snowy white. This is the result of dozens of washings over the years, initially by hand and then later by machine. It has kept its shape and shows virtually no sign of pilling despite years of hard wear – and it still feels as fresh and soft as the day it was made!

2 lbs (900 g) of cotton fibres were 'teased' and then given a few light strokes with the carders to make thick rolags. For the necessary high twist, I spun with a 10.5:1 wheel ratio on a single band wheel, using a short woollen draw. I wanted a thick textured yarn. The slubs or thicker areas in the yarn began and tapered off gradually: if very short thick slubs are made in cotton, the twist will always run over them and into the thinner sections, leaving an undertwisted slub. Cotton fibres are so short that they will soon work loose, causing pilling, soiling and weakness in the yarn. To make controlled slubs, pull back more slowly with the rolag hand, allowing the twist to catch up with more fibres. When the slub is thick enough, gradually quicken the draw, releasing fewer fibres to the twist.

The yarn was plied for strength, thickness and to balance the twist. For knitting purposes, a single thick cotton yarn does not work. The amount of twist needed for a balanced yarn, even after weighting, is not enough to stop the fibres working loose.

KNITTING PATTERN

For an average ladies size:
Tension: 10 sts to 5 cm (5 st to 1 inch).

Front:

With no. 9 ($3\frac{3}{4}$ mm) needles cast on 100 sts.
Beg. K row work 11 rows st st.
K for hemline.
Change to no. 7 ($4\frac{1}{2}$ mm) needles. Beg. K row work 4 rows st st.
Cord eyelet: K 46, cast off 4, K to end.
Cast on 4 sts above the 4 cast off.
Continue in st st until work measures 16 inches (41 cm) from hemline, ending after a P row.*
Shape armhole and divide for neck: cast off 12 sts.
K until there are 32 sts on needle after cast off. Turn.
Continue on these sts until armhole measures $5\frac{1}{2}$ inches (14 cm), ending after P row.
Shape neck: K 28 turn.
Leave remaining 4 sts on safety pin.
Continue on these st dec 1 sts at neck edge on every row to 22 sts.
Continue straight until armhole measures $7\frac{1}{2}$ inches (19 cm) ending after a P row.
Shape shoulder: cast off 7 sts at beg of next row and follow alt row.
Work one row.

76. A thick textured cotton yarn will knit into a very hardwearing garment

77.

Cast off remaining 8 sts.

With right side facing slip first 12 sts on safety pin, join yarn to rem sts and work to match first side, reversing shapings.

Back:

Omitting the cord eyelet work as front to*.

Shape armholes: cast off 12 sts at the beg of next 2 rows.

Continue straight until work matches front to shoulder ending after P row.

Shape shoulders: cast off 7 sts at beg of next 4 rows, 8 sts at beg of next 2 rows. Leave remaining 32 sts on a spare needle.

Sleeves:

With no. 9 ($3\frac{3}{4}$ mm) needles cast on 62 sts K 20 rows.

Change to no. 7 ($4\frac{1}{2}$ mm) needles. Beg K row cont in st st inc 1 st at both ends of 5th row and every foll 10th row to 78 st.

When work measures $14\frac{1}{2}$ inches (37 cm) change to garter st and cont until work measures $16\frac{1}{2}$ inches (42 cm).

Cast off.

Front borders:

Return to 12 sts at centre front.

With right side facing using no. 9 ($3\frac{3}{4}$ mm) needles K 6 rows on 1st 6 sts.

Make eyelet: K1, K2 tog, yf, yrn, K3.

K next row dropping extra loops.

K 6 rows.

Rep last 8 rows 5 times more, working 2 rows at end of last rep instead of 6 rows.

Slip sts on safety pin.

Rejoin yarn to rem sts and work to match the first side, working eyelet thus K3, yf, yrn, K2 tog, K1.

Neck band and hood:

Join shoulder seams.

With right side facing using no. 9 ($3\frac{3}{4}$ mm) needles K 6 sts on right front border, then 4 sts on right front, pick up and K 18 sts up right neck edge, K across st on back neck, pick up and K18 sts down left neck edge, 4 sts on safety pin, K 6 sts on left border (88 sts).

K3 rows.

K3, yf, yrn, K2 tog, K to last 3 st, yf, yrn, K 2 tog, K1.

K 1 row dropping extra loops.

K 2 rows.

K11 * inc 1 st, K 6, rep from * 10 times more, inc 1 st K to end (100 sts).

K 1 row.

Change to no. 7 ($4\frac{1}{2}$ mm) needles.

Make hood as follows:

K 1 row.

K 8, P to last 8 sts, K 8.

Rpt last 2 rows twice more.

K 49 sts, inc 1st, K 2, inc 1sts, K to end.

K 8, P to last 8 sts, K8.

Rep last 2 rows 3 times more.

K 50 sts, inc 1st, K 2, inc 1st, K to end.

Continue inc in this way on every foll 8th row to 112 sts.

Continue straight until work measures 13 inches (33 cm) from beg of hood, ending after wrong side row.

K 53, K 2 tog, K2, K 2 tog, tbl, K to end.

Work 3 rows straight.

K 52, K 2 tog, K 2, K 2 tog, tbl, K to end.

Continue dec in this way on foll 3 alt rows.

Work 1 row.

Cast off.

Join side and sleeve seams. Sew in sleeves. Join hood seam. Fold hem at lower edge to wrong side and slip stitch. Make twisted cords for lower edge and front inset.

19 Knitted and woven jacket

This eyecatching and much-admired jacket (see colour plate 4) is an ideal handspun, handwoven project and yet very simple to make. The yoke is knitted and the rest woven on a 20 inch (51 cm) rigid heddle loom. The 'meet and return' technique, using two weft threads, produces the striking pattern. One strip of fabric is woven for the body and the sleeves are woven to a paper pattern outline. The only cutting (and therefore wastage) is for two small semi-circles at the armholes.

I used a commercially spun 100 per cent camel hair warp, but found it slippery. Handspun wool would be easier to work with. The warp is not seen: all it has to be is strong and slightly hairy to form a cohesive fabric. It must be threaded through the heddle so that there is enough space for the handspun weft to bend round and cover the warp completely – in other words, it's a weft faced fabric.

Brown wool from a lustrous Jacob fleece and a dark Masham (semi-lustrous) and creamy-white

78.

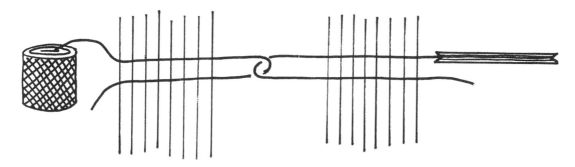

79. Meet and return technique

wool from a Masham were spun for the weft yarns. I carded the wool and rolled the webs lengthwise before spinning with a worsted draw using a 6.5:1 wheel ratio, which gave a shiny, softly twisted yarn. The brown wool was not blended, the different shades being spun randomly to give the darker vertical lines in the fabric. The white wool was spun to the same thickness as the brown.

When you have dressed the loom, spin a small sample of the weft to check that it will cover the warp, remembering that there are two weft yarns in every shed.

To begin weaving with the meet and return technique, wind the white weft on to a stick shuttle. Wind the brown yarn into a centre pull ball, and place it at the left side of the loom. If you do not have a ball winder place your hand wound ball in a bowl by the side of the loom to prevent it rolling about. Open the shed and take the stick shuttle from right to left. Pick up the brown weft and return the shuttle to the right, pulling the brown weft part way across the warp as in fig. 79. Close the shed and beat up the two weft yarns to cover the warp. Open the next shed and repeat the procedure, tucking the two ends into this shed. The brown may be pulled $\frac{1}{4}$ inch (1 cm) or nearly to the end of the warp, depending on the required design. For the jacket fabric most of my brown weft was pulled about half way across the

warp. You can make fine dotted lines by bringing the brown threequarters of the way across the shed, then following it with a brown taken only a short distance across. Wavy lines are made by taking two consecutive brown picks a long way across the shed, followed by a short brown. Spear-like points are made by taking the brown a little higher at each pick until the desired length is reached, then decreasing the distance of the brown at the same rate.

When you have woven 43 inches (109 cm) or your required body width, allowing for shrinkage, finish off and pack the warp with 2 inches (5 cm) of fabric strips, sticks, or card, before starting to weave the first sleeve (see fig. 80). I used a paper sleeve shape from a jacket sewing pattern, and wove an extra $\frac{1}{2}$ inch round this to allow for shrinkage. Put in another 2 inches (5 cm) of fabric strips between each sleeve. Take the material from the loom and zig zag, or oversew by hand, round the unfinished edges of the three woven pieces. Take out the strips and cut between each sleeve and the body. Wash, fulling slightly, then press whilst still damp.

After finishing the body measured 41 by $17\frac{1}{2}$ inches (104 by 45 cm) and the sleeves measured $17\frac{1}{2}$ by 19 inches (45 by 48 cm).

4 oz (110 g) of plied yarn was spun from the white Masham fleece to make the knitted yoke.

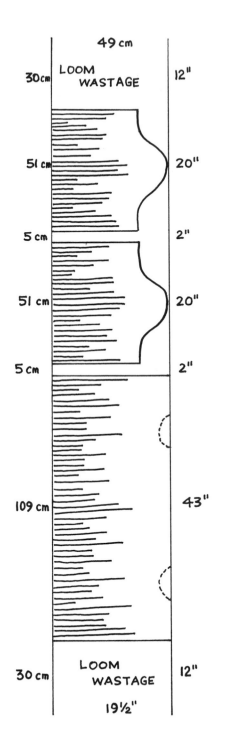

49 cm

30cm LOOM WASTAGE

51 cm

5 cm

51 cm

5 cm

109 cm

30 cm LOOM WASTAGE

19½"

12"

20"

2"

20"

2"

43"

12"

80.

KNITTED YOKE PATTERN

Tension: 6 stitches to one inch (12 stitches to 5 cm) 6 rows to one inch (12 rows to 5 cm)

Right front: With no. 8 (4 mm) knitting needle pick up 43 sts evenly along 6¾ inches (17 cm of the long white edge of material as shown in fig. 81 by pushing a crochet hook through the fabric. Continue in st st for 4 inches (10 cm).

To shape neck: cast off 7 sts at neck edge.

Continue in st st dec 1 st at neck edge on every row until the work measures 5½ inches (14 cm), 27 sts.

Cast off 9 sts at shoulder edge and k to end of row. P 18 sts.

Cast off 9 sts at shoulder edge and K to end of row. P 9 sts.

Cast off remaining stitches.

Pick up 43 sts on the other end of the body fabric.

Complete second half of front yoke to match the first.

Back yoke: starting 12¾ inches (31 cm) from front edge pick up 99 sts evenly along 16½ inches (42 cm) of fabric as shown in fig. 81.

Continue in st st for 5½ inches (14 cm).

Cast off 9 sts at shoulder edge.

K 21 sts, k 2 tog turn. Cont on these sts only.

P 2 tog, p to end (20 sts).

Cast off 9 sts, k to last 2 sts, k 2 tog.

P 2 tog, p to end.

Cast off remaining 10 sts.

Rejoin yarn to work and cast off centre 35 sts.

Shape second back shoulder as the first.

Join shoulder seams.

To make picot neck band: pick up 76 sts evenly around neck (not including the first 3 and last 3 cast off stitches, which are the hem).

K 6 rows of st st.

* K 2 tog, make 1 * repeat from * to * to end of row.

P 1 row.

St st 6 rows.

Cast off.

Fold over picot hem and slip stitch into position leaving the ends open for a cord to be inserted.

Mark the position of the sleeves on the body piece

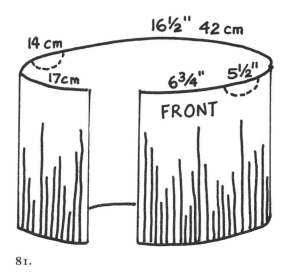

81.

and zig zag or oversew a curved shape 2 inches (5 cm) deep and $5\frac{1}{2}$ inches (14 cm) across as shown in fig. 81. Go over the stitching before cutting out the semi-circle shapes. Sew the sleeve seams, making flat seams. Sew the sleeves into the armholes easing in a little fullness at the sleeve head. Turn back about a $\frac{1}{4}$ inch (1 cm) on the front edges and three stitches on the yoke sections, and slip stitch to the inside forming a neat hem. It is advisable to bind the armhole seams. Sew in a zip and make a twisted cord to thread through the neck band. I threaded a large needle with three lengths of plied yarn and sewed a row of large back stitches over the shoulder and front yoke seams. These stitches were pulled up slightly to give a gathered effect to the front yokes.

20 Woven rug

Sarah was a pet sheep of unusual parentage: the ram was a Rough Fell and the ewe a Jacob. Sarah's long and coarse fleece ranged from black to grey. This wool was combined with mid to light grey wool from a two-year-old Herdwick ewe to make a shaded rug 77 by $36\frac{1}{2}$ inches (196 by 91 cm) woven on a 40 inch (102 cm) four shaft jack loom.

Jack looms are not ideal for weaving thick rugs because the rising shed method, like that of most table looms, does not allow extreme warp tension. Counterbalanced and countermarche looms have sheds in which some warp ends rise and others fall. Less strain is put on the warp to make a good shed and so a high warp tension can

be applied. I had planned a tabby weave for this rug, but discovered that only a thin weft would cover the warp. This meant that the rug would have been too flimsy for floor use and take a long time to weave. But weaving a 2/2 twill allowed for a much thicker weft yarn to be packed down tightly, giving a heavy rug.

Both fleeces were skirted and then washed. When dry, they were divided in half, lengthways. Working on one half of Sarah's fleece, I sorted out the darkest wool and this was spun first. Gradually, the lighter shades of the fleece were blended in until threequarters of this half fleece had been spun. Next, small amounts of dark wool from half of the Herdwick fleece were introduced into the

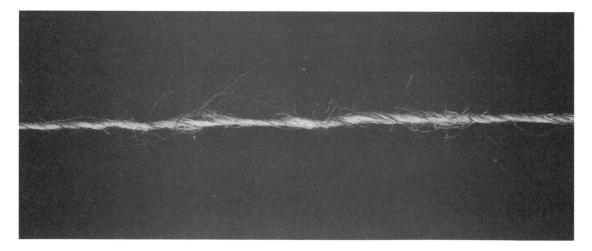

82.

yarn, so that wool was blended gradually from black to grey, using up the remaining quarter. Now, one half of the Herdwick fleece was treated in the same way – spinning the mid-grey wool first and ending with the paler grey. The remaining half Herdwick and half Sarah fleeces were treated in exactly the opposite way, i.e. first working on the lighter portions.

Both fleeces were very 'open' and a delight to spin. They needed no carding at all. Chunks of fleece were pulled off and spun on an Indian wheel, ratio 2.9:1, using a worsted draw. The slow ratio gave me ample time to tease out the fleece with my left hand as I spun. When blending, often I had two lots of wool of different shades on my knee and spun them alternately.

After spinning some 10 oz (280 g) I began weaving so that I could check whether the shading was right. A ski-shuttle, when filled with $4\frac{1}{2}$ oz (130 g) of weft yarn wove 4 inches (10 cm) and took about 30 minutes to weave.

The subtle shades of natural colours on this very hardwearing rug (it has been machine-washed successfully) give an effect which can only be achieved by using handspun yarns.

21 Shaded garments

The handspinner has a big advantage in being able to make a yarn exactly as needed for a particular project. Shaded garments are a fine example of this. The careful blending of colours in the yarn can result in a distinctive garment which no machine can match. Any colours can be used in this technique, but natural shades look particularly effective (see colour plate 5).

There are two ways of producing the colour gradation. One is a subtle change from one shade to the next, whereas the other gives a more speckled colour change.

The first method involves teasing and careful blending of colours on the carders. The more the effort put in at the rolag stage, the more subtle the shading will be. To make a plied yarn, the two singles must have the same number of shaded rolags. It's easier to plan the project if you make two lines of rolags, each line representing one singles yarn. For example, a 13 oz (370 g) jumper made from a Jacob fleece half white and half dark brown had two lines of rolags for the body comprising:

First singles	*Second singles*
5 brown	7 brown
4 brown with 1% white	2 brown with 1% white
4 brown with 10% white	2 brown with 5% white
5 brown with 30% white	7 brown with 30% white

9 brown with 50% white	9 brown with 50% white
5 white with 30% brown	7 white with 30% brown
4 white with 10% brown	2 white with 5% brown
4 white with 1% brown	2 white with 1% brown
	2 white

plied together

This may be simplified as:

9 brown rolags
9 brown rolags with white flecks
9 brown rolags with 50% white   } × 2 for a plied yarn
9 white rolags with brown flecks
white rolags

If you work out the approximate weight of the jumper body and then weigh the rolags, you can arrange it so that the shading finishes half way or one third of the way up the garment. Another way to check the extent of colour gradation is to start knitting the garment as soon as you have spun a ball. After knitting a few inches you may decide the gradation is too sudden, in which case add more rolags of the appropriate shades to the two lines. Always avoid having too many seams and matching problems by knitting the front and back in one piece to the armholes. Having completed the main body of the jumper, it is easy to estimate the number of rolags needed in the sleeve shading – about a third.

Knitting a scarf with this technique is a good way to begin. The one illustrated in colour plate 5 was made from:

2 black rolags
4 black rolags with white specks
4 black rolags with 50% white
4 white rolags with black specks   × 2 for
8 white rolags   a plied
4 white rolags with black specks   yarn
4 white rolags with 50% black
4 black rolags with white specks
2 black rolags

The second method does not involve such thorough blending and the colours are mixed mainly in spinning. Don't think in terms of the number of rolags, but in the number of full bobbins required for a project. For example, half a bobbin is filled with a black singles, then white introduced in small sections by spinning with two rolags – one black and the other white – side by side on your knee. As the bobbin fills, the white sections become longer. Only when the yarn is in the 50% white, 50% black stage do I roughly card the two colours together before spinning.

This is not a particularly easy method for the novice spinner because it involves many joins, all of which must be as strong as the main yarn. It is, however, a good method to use when you have a fleece or two fleeces of equal quality which are suitable for spinning straight from the fleece. Two pieces of fleece are kept on the knee and spun from alternately.

My favourite handspun garment is a heavy jacket, knitted or crocheted, with a shaded body, sleeves and hood in natural fleece colours. Its distinctive design depends entirely on the handspinner's art, not on the skills of the dyer or knitter. And this is surely what handspinning is all about.

22 Shetland stoles

Shawls and stoles made by the Shetland Islanders are gossamer fine and look like intricate spiders' webs. A stole made in the traditional way, handspun and hand knitted will become a family heirloom, so it is worthwhile learning to spin a yarn as finely as possible. There are many points to consider in making such a yarn: the condition of your hands, the most suitable fleece, a well-adjusted wheel, fleece preparation, the spinning method, the pattern, and the finishing of the stole.

Shetland shawls, scarves and stoles became fashionable and were sold to the wealthy, the proceeds being used to buy supplies for the islanders. Even when times were hard and everyone needed to work a long day, the Shetland lace knitters did not do any rough work around the croft: it was considered more important that their hands be kept smooth. Take extra care with your hands because it is so easy to snag a fine yarn with rough skin. This is your excuse to put aside all unpleasant chores for a while!

For an extra fine yarn you will need to find an extra fine fleece. You will be investing many hours of time on this project, so it is worth taking your time choosing one. Merino, Merino Cross and Southdown are excellent. Also suitable are the shoulder areas of fine fleeces, 56's and above, such as white Shetland. Merino wool has many crimps, which help in spinning a fine thread, and can be made into a semi-worsted or woollen yarn.

The Southdown has shorter, more bouncy wool which lends itself to woollen spinning, but when washed fluffs up more than Merino, giving the appearance of a slightly thicker yarn.

My black stole was made from a singles yarn from the shoulder wool of a black Suffolk. It was the finest fleece I had at the time and I was eager to make a start. But it would have been wiser to wait for a finer fleece.

I have spun on many wheels. Some are impossible for spinning ultra fine yarns, namely bobbin-driven ones because the pull-in rate is too fierce. Bobbin-braked wheels, like the Ashford, need to be well oiled, the drive band must be on the smallest flyer groove and the tension brake as slack as possible. If you are using a heavy nylon wire for braking, try a lighter wire or cord and let this sit loosely on the bobbin. It is always better to splice or sew the driving band, and for this project it is essential. A knot causes bumps, noticeable when fine spinning. Nylon bands are a good idea. They can be bought in different weights and are joined by heating the two ends over a flame, then rolled quickly together with moistened fingers to give a smooth join.

For spinning ultra fine yarns I think double band wheels, such as a little Shetland upright wheel, give slightly more control than single band wheels. My favourite wheel for this kind of project is one that gives me the minimum pull-in tension, plenty of twist and effortless treadling. It

84. Ultra-fine Merino stole, knitted on size 12 ($2\frac{3}{4}$ mm) and size 14 (2mm) needles, and stole knitted from black Suffolk wool

is an old double band Scandinavian wheel, with a 26 inch (66 cm) wheel diameter. I have a collection of different sized spindle whorls for it, and use the one which is only a little larger in diameter than the bobbin groove. This allows maximum slippage and minimum pull-in tension. The wheel ratio is 12:1.

The spindle whorl should have a V-shaped groove to enable the drive band to grip, whereas the bobbin should have a U-shaped groove to allow the band to slip and give you full control of the pull-in tension. If using a double band wheel, slide the mother-of-all down the stock until the band slips round both bobbin and whorl – it will

make a wheezing noise – then slowly tighten until the band is just taut enough to drive the spindle whorl, leaving the bobbin to slip. If you have only one whorl for a double band wheel and the difference in diameter of bobbin and whorl is too great, try spinning with the bobbin half filled. The larger the yarn package becomes, the less the rate of take-up. It will take many yards to fill half a bobbin with such fine thread, so in this instance there is little disadvantage in using only half the bobbin. To summarise, whichever wheel you use, it should by well oiled, the band smoothly joined, and it should give the minimum pull tension and high twist.

85.

Unless your chosen fleece is fresh and very clean, wash it. After all, the yarn will be the thickness of only a few fibres and if grease makes two or three stick together, this is two or three too many. The shorter the wool staple, the more grease it has. Merino is so greasy that it requires special washing. Tie the locks together with sewing cotton in groups of two or three and add washing soda (half a teaspoonful to two pints of water) to your washing solution of detergent or soap. Leave for an hour, then rinse and repeat the wash, leaving it to soak for a further two or three hours. Throughout the process, handle the tied staples very gently.

For woollen spinning, make thin rolags no bigger than your finger. Ideally, the carders should have closely spaced teeth, similar to cotton carders. If you use ordinary carders, brush very lightly keeping the fibres on top of the teeth. For worsted draw, tease out or comb each lock, starting at the tip and working towards the middle, then turning over and combing the other end.

Whichever spinning method you use, the yarn must have plenty of twist. Only the twist holds the yarn together, as it cannot rely on bulk of fibre for strength. Before starting, so that you can see what you're doing more easily, place a contrasting cloth over your knee and floor. When woollen spinning, hold the rolag very loosely, as fine fibres compress easily. With the long draw method you will need to treadle quickly at the end of the draw to get sufficient twist.

The Shetland Islanders used a modified worsted draw to make their ultra fine yarns. Separate a small bunch of fibres from a combed lock. A whole lock, especially of Merino wool, is too much to hold at once because your hand will become hot and the fibres will compress and stick together. It is usual to spin worsted yarn from the cut end of a lock, but for a fine yarn spin from the tips so that the scales may link with those of adjacent fibres and help to form a cohesive yarn. The front hand draws out the fibres to about the length of the staple and then rolls them in the opposite direction of the twist with the thumb and index finger. This enables the fibres to be drawn out further before letting the twist run down. It is a continuous drawing and rolling action. Some spinners find it helps to rub a little oil on the fingers when spinning washed wool. If the yarn breaks, pull it out at least 8 inches (20 cm) from the orifice before joining. As you begin treadling, let the yarn creep slowly towards the orifice, joining as you do so. This will lessen any tug from the wheel and prevent further breakage.

Examine the yarn carefully after you have spun a few feet and check that it has enough twist. A fine singles is more difficult to get right than a plied one. The yarn needs enough twist to make it sufficiently strong for knitting, yet remaining soft. Too much twist will make the yarn hard or so kinky that the twist cannot be set. It is better to leave a fine singles on the wheel for a few days to set the twist rather than attempting to wind it into a hank for washing and weighting.

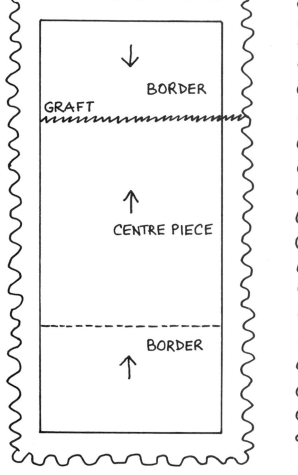
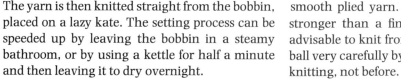

86. Arrows indicate direction knitting is worked

87. Arrows indicate direction knitting is worked

The yarn is then knitted straight from the bobbin, placed on a lazy kate. The setting process can be speeded up by leaving the bobbin in a steamy bathroom, or by using a kettle for half a minute and then leaving it to dry overnight.

If making a plied yarn, remember to add just as much twist in the plying process to obtain a balanced yarn. It's easy to think you don't need much twist to put together such highly twisted singles, and then find you have two yarns loosely wrapped around each other instead of one,

smooth plied yarn. A fine plied yarn is usually stronger than a fine singles, but even so it is advisable to knit from the bobbin, or wind into a ball very carefully by hand, always washing after knitting, not before.

There are many traditional Shetland lace knitting patterns. Each family tended to make variations to the local stitch pattern. A number of books have been published recently featuring a good choice of stitch patterns (see bibliography) and usually include examples of both lace stitches and border patterns. In this way you can choose your own combination and made a truly unique garment.

A stole is made in three pieces: a centre piece and border, another border, and a lace edge. The second border is grafted on to the centre piece, and the edge laced or sewn to the finished piece (see fig. 86). But if you choose a centre piece with a one-way design, it will have to be worked as shown in fig. 87 and grafted in the middle.

Always cast on very loosely and keep the tension loose to prevent the yarn breaking. Initially, the knitting should look very loose. It is stretching which brings out the full beauty of the lace pattern. It is always wise to knit samples of the patterns you intend to use.

My black stole weighs less than 1 oz (25 g) and measures 20 by 45 inches (51 by 114 cm) and was knitted on no. 10 ($3\frac{1}{4}$ mm) needles, with 100 stitches cast on for the borders and centre piece.

After knitting and grafting, the stole should be washed gently in warm soap or detergent solution and left to soak for an hour. After rinsing it should be laid out flat on a towel and rolled to remove excess moisture. Shetland Islanders pegged out their gossamer fine shawls and stoles to dry on grassy hillsides. I use a piece of board covered with polystyrene tiles on which to pin damp shawls, but a clean sheet on the carpet would do. Use stainless steel pins, pinning all round under moderate tension at first. Then move each pin back to tighten. Pay special attention to the scalloped or pointed edges. The yarn will stretch further as it dries. Leave it for a few days until it is thoroughly dry and set. If you wash the stole again, it will have to be pinned out in this way.

23 Embroidered cardigan

Dyeing with plants is intriguing and enjoyable, more so because the results are unpredictable. The unique colours you will obtain depend on factors such as the type of soil in which the plant grew, how much sunshine it got, when you gathered it and the nature of your local water supply. Occasionally, the results are disappointing. My first attempt was with dandelions and alum, said to produce a superb yellow. My children picked a bucketful of brilliant yellow dandelion flowers, but all I ended up with was a rather nasty grey colour. To hide my disappointment, I raided the spice cupboard and added turmeric.

But one source that never fails and is readily available throughout the year is onion skins. This cardigan (see colour plate 6), made from Suffolk fleece, shows the variety of shades that can be obtained from onion skins. Some of the wool was dyed without a mordant, and the rest with either alum, chrome or tin. The variety of onion influences the final colour: one batch I used was a very deep and rich tan colour, which produced good results on the unmordanted wool. I was delighted to discover that greengrocers de-skin large onions before displaying them and are usually happy to supply the skins. I collect mine in the nylon mesh sacks the onions come in and, as these withstand boiling, simply weigh them and put the sackful of skins in an enamel bucket for an hour's boiling.

I use roughly equal proportions of onion skins and fleece. 3 to 4 oz (85 to 110 g) of alum (potassium aluminium sulphate) plus $\frac{3}{4}$ to 1 oz (20 to 30 g) cream of tartar is added for each pound (450 g) of wool and simmered for between 45 and 60 minutes. Alum mordanted wool seems to improve with keeping, so it is wise to mordant more than you need.

Chrome is light sensitive so wool mordanted with this should be used straight away. I use between $\frac{1}{4}$ and $\frac{1}{2}$ oz (7 to 14 g) of chrome (potassium dichromate) to 1 lb (450 g) of wool and simmer for 45 to 60 minutes.

To brighten the colour, whichever mordant has been used, I add about $\frac{1}{2}$ oz of tin (stannous chloride) for every pound of wool 15 minutes before the end of dyeing. Lift the fleece out, add the tin and stir well before putting the fleece back. Simmer for 15 to 20 minutes.

Wool of varying shades can be obtained by removing a third of the wool from the dyebath after 15 minutes simmering, another third after 15 minutes more and the remainder 15 minutes later.

14 oz (400 g) of wool was used for the cardigan. It was blended well and carded as described in project 21. Chrome mordanted wool of a dark, gingery tan merged into alum mordanted orange, which in turn merged into an unmordanted pale peach colour, and then to white. The fleece was quite short and bouncy and

plied yarn was soon made, spinning long draw on a 10.5:1 wheel ratio.

Fine single yarns were spun for the embroidery. The brightest of the embroidered daisies were those from yarn dyed with the addition of tin to the bath. The palest colours were from an exhausted dye bath and some unmordanted wool.

Some years and several washings later, the cardigan is just as it was made: none of the colours have faded, nor has the dye run from the flowers into the white wool.

24 Colourful crocheted coat

This colourful, easily-made jacket is what I have always imagined the Biblical 'coat of many colours' to be like (see colour plate 7). It comprises every conceivable natural shade of wool: all those leftover bits from other projects. My jacket was made from the wool of half a dozen or more different breeds. You don't need a spinning wheel either, which makes this an ideal project for the novice spinner or those wishing to learn the technique of using a Navajo spindle to spin a thick singles yarn.

Unlike the drop spindle, the Navajo spindle is very long – about 36 inches (91 cm) – and works by rolling it along the thigh. It consists of a shaft tapered at both ends, with a whorl positioned some 8 inches (20 cm) from the bottom 4 to 6 inches (10 to 15 cm) in diameter (fig. 88). You can make your own Navajo spindle from a length of dowel and a paint tin lid or something similar. Make sure you cut the hole in the exact centre of the whorl, otherwise it will not spin properly. You can, of course, also spin a thick singles yarn on a wheel with a low ratio and large orifice.

Choose a fleece with different colours, such as a Jacob, or collect around 2 lbs (1 kg) from various fleeces of similar quality. Make thick rolags and put them in piles according to colour. Spin the rolags randomly, but if you have only small amounts of some colours then plan things so that you can space out these yarns throughout the garment.

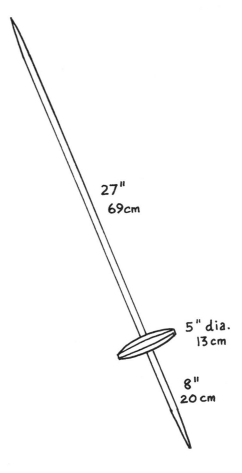

88. Navajo spindle

89.

Sit on a low chair or stool and practise twisting the spindle by rolling it along your thigh from the knee upwards. Use the flat of your hand to do this until you reach the top of the thigh. Then encircle the spindle while it is still rotating with your thumb and index finger (fig. 89) and take it back to the knee to begin the action once more. Before long you will find it easy to get the spindle spinning quickly in a continuous action.

Tie a leader yarn of about 48 inches (122 cm) just above the whorl. Then spiral it up the shaft by twisting the spindle clockwise, leaving a

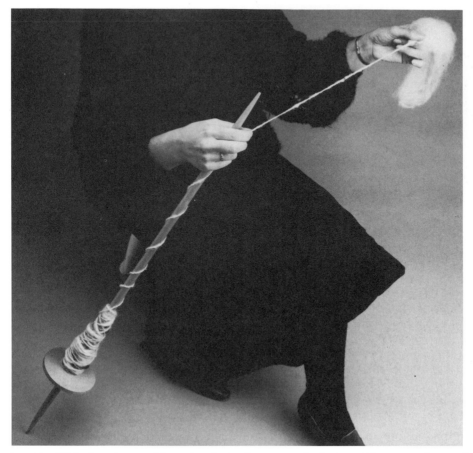

90.

length of 8 inches (20 cm) hanging from the top. Join the rolag by overlapping the leader yarn about 2 inches (5 cm). Spin the spindle and let the twist run up the leader yarn and catch onto a few fibres from the rolag. Having joined on, the left thumb and index finger should hold firmly at the point where the twist runs out. Roll the spindle until plenty of twist has built up on the yarn.

Now hold the top of the spindle and at the same time grip the yarn at the spindle tip with the thumb and index finger of the right hand. Draw back the rolag with the left hand just ahead of the twist, stopping when the twist is insufficient to make a cohesive yarn (fig. 90). If lumps occur, a sharp tug often evens out the yarn. Spin until the left arm is outstretched.

Back the yarn off the spindle by holding it at an angle away from you, and turning it anti-clockwise. Now wind on the yarn, twisting clockwise, forming a cone shape above the whorl. Leave enough yarn to spiral up to the spindle top and a few inches hanging free.

If you find your yarn becoming too fine you are pulling back too fast for the twist to catch sufficient fibres. Try pulling back more slowly, or building up more twist, i.e. rolling the spindle more times on your thigh. If the yarn is too thick, draw back faster, presenting fewer fibres to the twist, or reduce the number of times you roll the spindle before drawing out.

These movements may seem slow and jerky at first, but with a little practice it will become a smooth, continuous action. Wind the yarn into hanks. Wash it, or soak for a few minutes if it is already washed, then hang to dry with a weight attached to set the twist.

91.

PATTERN

Size: medium ladies

Tension: 7 tr to 4 inches or 14 tr to 10 cm.

With no. 1 (8 mm) crochet hook make 72 chain.

1 tr in 3rd chain from hook, 1 tr in each chain to end (70 tr).

Continue in tr until work measures 13 inches (33 cm).

Right front and sleeve: 17 tr, make 31 chain turn.

1 tr, in 3rd chain from hook tr, to end (45 tr).

Continue on these sts in tr, until work measures 10 inches (25 cm) from armhole.

Sl st over 4 sts at neck edge, work tr to end of row.

Tr to last 2 tr, break yarn and fasten off.

Left front and sleeve: Repeat as for right side, reversing shapings.

Back: Rejoin yarn to middle strand make 31 chain, turn.

1 tr in 3rd chain from hook, tr above each chain, and across 36 tr of back, make 31 chain.

Work in tr on these 92 sts until work measures same as front from armhole to shoulder.

Break yarn, fasten off.

Sew shoulder and underarm seams.

Work 2 rows in dc up front edges and round neck using no. 4 (6 mm) crochet hook.

With a contrast yarn work 4 rows dc at sleeve cuff, dec 1st on each row.

With a contrast yarn make 3 twisted cords and thread through the dc spaces at neck edge and cuffs.

Make 6 small tassels and attach to cords.

Insert zip (the large toothed plastic type works well).

25 Novelty yarn jumper

Unlike some novelty yarns, this unusual one lends itself to knitted fabric. The jumper (fig. 92), knitted on large wooden needles, has soft knobbly patches and open lacy areas. It looks particularly effective when worn over something of a contrasting colour.

I used a Texel fleece, but any soft, medium staple wool is suitable. It was spun on a wheel with a jumbo flyer attachment. If you don't have a large flyer then you will need to stop and guide the thicker slubs through a small orifice, or simply scale down the size of the slubs.

First of all, 24 oz (680 g) of wool was carded into rolags. The first singles yarn was spun with an S twist (wheel anti-clockwise) using a worsted draw and a 4.3:1 wheel ratio. This ratio was a little low, so I treadled quickly to produce a fine, even yarn.

The second singles is the slub yarn. This is spun with a Z twist with the same wheel ratio, but treadling slower. Long slubs – some up to 15 inches (38 cm) – were made between roughly equal lengths of fine, even yarn. Use a worsted draw to make the slubs. Draft out more fibres by pinching at the base of the drafting triangle and drawing forwards. My slubs were fat enough to pass easily through a $\frac{5}{8}$ inch orifice. Most of the twist will run on to the thinner parts of the yarn, so it is important to smooth the slubs as you spin, tucking in any stray fibres. If odd tufts of fibres are left hanging out from a slub the twist will be insufficient to keep them in place and they will eventually work loose and cause pilling.

The two singles are then plied with an S twist. This has the effect of overtwisting the finer yarn, causing it to bite into the soft slubs making a bead or knobbly effect. A shiny, rather hard yarn is made between the slubs. After hanking, the yarn was washed and then dried with a weight attached.

About $2\frac{1}{2}$ oz (70 g) of fine, even plied yarn is spun for the picot neck and lower edging.

PATTERN

Size: average woman's

Tension: 8 sts to $4\frac{3}{4}$ inches (8 sts to 12 cm) approx 6 rows to 2 inches.

Back and front: using no.00 (9 mm) long wooden needles cast on 66 sts.

Continue in st st for 13 inches (33 cm).

Divide front for neck – K 15 sts K2 tog. Turn.

Work to end of 16 sts.

Sleeve: cast on 25 sts. Turn.

Continue on these 41 sts dec 1 st at neck edge every foll 6th row 4 times (37 sts).

Continue straight until work measures 8 inches from first neck dec.

Slip sts on to a holder, or thread a length of string through.

Rejoin yarn to centre neck dec and K second half of front to match first, reversing shapings. Slip

92. Novelty yarn jumper from a soft, medium staple wool

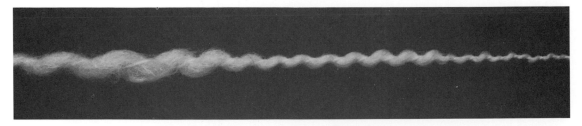

93.

sts on to holder or string.

Back: Join yarn to armhole edge. K 1 row, cast on 25 sts.

Work 58 sts, then cast on 25 sts.

Continue in st st on these 83 sts until back measures same as front.

K 37 sts cast off 9, K 36 sts.

At this point, decide which is to be the right side. I used the rough face as this emphasises the slubs, but both sides are attractive. Graft the shoulder and upper sleeve seams.

Neck edge: with right side facing, using the fine, even yarn and 4 no. 9 ($3\frac{3}{4}$ mm) needles, pick up 107 sts evenly round neck edge.

Dec 1 st at centre neck and K 105 sts.

Cont in st st dec 1 st at neck centre over next 6 rows.

* K 2 tog yf * repeat from * to * to end.

P 1 row.

Cont in st st for 7 rows inc 1 st at neck centre on each row.

Cast off.

Fold back picot neck edge and sl st into position on inside.

Lower edge: Using fine yarn and no. 9 ($3\frac{3}{4}$ mm) needles pick up 112 sts evenly over lower edge of front and back.

Work 7 rows in st st.

* K2 tog, yf * repeat from * to * end.

P 1 row.

Work 7 rows in st st.

Cast off. Sew side seam.

Sl st picot hem into position.

Sleeve cuffs: with large needles and right side facing (mine was rough side) pick up 32 sts evenly round cast off edge.

With novelty yarn k 1 row.

St st 5 more rows.

Cast off.

Repeat for second sleeve.

Sew underarm sleeve seams.

Fold back cuffs and stitch at seam.

26 Loopy body warmer

This indigo-dyed, knitted loopy body warmer is an ideal partner for the ever-popular blue denim jeans or skirt. Dyeing with indigo is like performing a trick: only when the wool is lifted from the greenish-yellow liquid and exposed to the air does it slowly turn blue (colour plate 2).

I made mine from 18 oz (510 g) of Lonk fleece which was carded, the webs rolled lengthwise, and spun with a 6.5:1 wheel ratio into a medium to thick singles yarn. Because of the wool's long staple – around 5 inches (13 cm) – it was spun with a worsted draw, giving slightly more twist than that necessary to hold the yarn together. Stray fibres were stroked back into the yarn with the front hand as it was being spun. A good pull-in tension was needed to prevent over-twisting. The yarn was made into hanks with three good ties, and then washed to remove all traces of grease. The wool must be thoroughly wet before dyeing, so the work was planned to enable me to dye the same day as washing was completed, leaving the hanks soaking until ready to dye.

Indigo is insoluble in water, so a special dyeing method has to be followed. When oxygen is removed with sodium hydrosulphite, it is known as indigo white. In this form it will dissolve in an alkaline solution, in this case made with caustic soda. It becomes a greenish-yellow liquid. After the fibres have been penetrated, they become indigo blue on exposure to the air. Because indigo is insoluble in water, it will not wash out and is

94.

very fast to light. But it does tend to rub off, especially on cotton, hence the pale patches on the knees of jeans.

This recipe uses synthetic indigo, which contains no impurities and is four times stronger than natural indigo. The method is the same, whichever you use (the natural stuff is quite expensive now) and as it is more involved than some dyeing methods it makes sense to dye as much yarn or fleece as possible.

Begin by making the indigo stock solution which, if stored in a tightly sealed jar, will keep for many weeks.

INDIGO STOCK SOLUTION

1 oz (30 g) synthetic indigo, or four times the amount of natural indigo.

$2\frac{3}{4}$ oz (83 g) sodium hydrosulphite, also known as sodium dithionite.

3 oz (90 g) sodium hydroxide – caustic soda.

Method

1. In a separate container, make a caustic solution. Always add caustic to water and protect yourself from burns. You need just enough water to dissolve the caustic soda.
2. Put the indigo in a gallon jar.
3. Add the caustic solution to the indigo and mix well.
4. Fill up the gallon jar with hot water 120°–130°F (50° to 55°C) and not more than 140°F (60°C).
5. Sprinkle sodium hydrosulphite on the surface. Do not stir.
6. Let it stand for an hour.
7. Test with a glass rod. The liquid should be a clear yellow green which turns blue on the rod in 30 seconds. If there are white specks on the glass, add a little more caustic solution. If there are blue specks the indigo still contains oxygen, so add a little more sodium hydrosulphite.

You can use a smaller jar with less hot water, but this more concentrated stock should be used more sparingly.

DYEING WITH INDIGO

First prepare the dyebath. I use a plastic kitchen refuse bin, but a large bucket would do. Insulate the bath by tying several layers of newspaper round it, which helps to maintain the temperature around 120°F (50°C).

Fill the dyebath threequarters full with hot water between 120° and 130°F (50° to 55°C) but never exceeding 140°F (60°C) or the dyebath will be spoiled. I used 3 gallons (4.5 litres) in my refuse bin.

Sprinkle a teaspoonful of sodium hydrosulphite over the surface. Leave for 10 minutes and do not stir.

Carefully pour $1\frac{1}{2}$ to 2 pints (0.85 to 1.1 litres) of the indigo stock solution into the dyebath. Great care must be taken to avoid introducing oxygen. This means gentle stirring, no drips and no bubbles.

Stir gently, not breaking the surface. Loop the hanks together on a piece of cord. Enter the thoroughly wetted wool in the dyebath, avoiding drips. Leave it for 20 minutes, moving it gently around only once. Wearing rubber gloves, carefully remove the hanks, letting them drip into another container and not the dyebath. Sprinkle on another teaspoonful of sodium hydrosulphite to keep the bath yellow. Open out the hanks and as the oxygen in the air meets them, the yellowish green yarn will become blue.

Air the wool for at least 30 minutes.

Colour and fastness is built up by repeated dippings and airings, so even if you want a pale shade you should dip at least twice to make it fast. After the first dipping and airing subsequent dips can be of 15 minutes with 10 minutes airing. If the colour is not deep enough, add a little more stock before adding the teaspoonful of sodium hydrosulphite.

When you have the depth of colour you want, air the wool for one or two days. To neutralise the harmful effects of alkali (caustic soda), the yarn must be soaked in water with a small amount of acetic acid (or larger amount of vinegar) for about half an hour. Then rinse it in clean water.

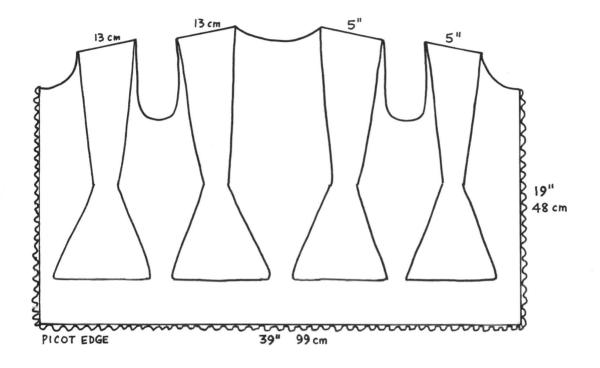

13 cm   13 cm   5"   5"

19"
48 cm

PICOT EDGE   39"   99 cm

95.

For the body warmer, I had nine skeins, weighing 20 oz (570 g). Two were dipped twice to give a pale blue. The rest were dipped five times in all to give a deep, rich blue. At this stage, the contents of the dyebath had reduced considerably and the liquid had cooled.

Another teaspoon of sodium hydrosulphite was added to the bath and left for 15 minutes. About 16 oz (450 g) of leftover discoloured bits of fleece were added as an experiment. They were removed from the cool bath after 45 minutes and aired for half and hour. The process was repeated, giving a surprisingly good shade which covered the yellowy stains. The wool was rather patchily dyed, but needed only blending and carding to produce an evenly-coloured yarn. For effect, I spun after the minimum of carding to give a mottled yarn.

BODY WARMER

The body warmer has a picot hem worked in stocking stitch and is then knitted in a loop stitch. Most of the garment is knitted with the deeper coloured yarn. The pale yarn was divided into four and knitted in four triangle shapes (fig. 95). Some of the mottled yarn was knitted into long triangle shapes at the shoulders. A picot edge was made on the fronts and around the neck edge.

A singles yarn must be balanced for use in a loop stitch fabric. If it is not, tight spikes will form instead of soft loops. If, after weighting the dyed yarn the hank still curls slightly in the direction of the twist, make it into a folded hank. Twist it between both hands in the opposite direction to the yarn twist. Leave it like this for a day and then it will be ready for knitting.

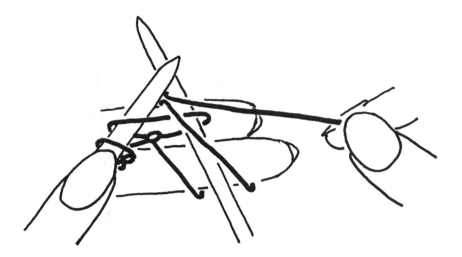

96. Knitted loop stitch

LOOP STICH

This is a useful stitch not only for body warmers, but for waistcoats and jackets too.

Row 1: K
Row 2: K 1, * insert needle into next st, place first 2 fingers of left hand under needle, wind yarn clockwise round needle and fingers twice, then over needle once. Pull all loops through and place on left hand needle, K loops together with st * . Repeat from * to * to last st K 1. These two rows form pattern. See fig. 96.

For a less dense fabric three knit rows can be made between each loop row, or wind one loop round fingers once.

27 Edge to edge cardigans

A thick singles yarn and a fine plied yarn are combined in these cardigans (see colour plate 8): the yarns knitted together in one garment give an interesting contrast in texture. The brown cardigan is made from a brown and white Jacob fleece and the purple cardigan from Suffolk fleece dyed with elderberries.

The Jacob fleece was skirted and a coarse, hairy section removed from the britch area. The remaining wool was then sorted for colour, making a pile of brown wool of different shades and a pile of white wool. A small quantity of brown was teased roughly with the white and the rest of the brown teased and mixed thoroughly to give a uniform colour. Some 13 oz (370 g) of the white/beige wool was carded into large rolags. It was spun into a soft, thick singles yarn on a wheel with a jumbo flyer, ratio 4.3:1, using a worsted draw. The yarn was washed and dried with a weight attached to set the twist. About 9 oz (255 g) of brown wool was carded and finely spun using a long draw technique with a 10.5:1 wheel ratio. The two brown singles were then plied to give a balanced yarn.

1 lb of elderberries were picked to dye 1 lb (450 g) of Suffolk wool which first had been mordanted with alum. After 20 minutes simmering, a teaspoonful of stannous chloride was added to the dyebath and the wool simmered a further 10 minutes. The wool became a deep, rich purple and was left to cool overnight. It was taken out

next morning, but because the dye bath still had plenty of colour I decided to use it again. A further 11 oz (310 g) of alum mordanted Suffolk wool was simmered for 30 minutes to give a pale lavender colour.

All the lavender wool was carded and then spun on a jumbo flyer, producing a soft, thick irregular yarn, the thickest bits of which would just pass through the jumbo orifice. After hanking, it was soaked for 10 minutes and hung to dry with a weight attached. About half the purple wool was carded and spun, using the long draw technique, making a fine even yarn which was then plied.

The fine, purple yarn was knitted in st st with the smooth side as the right side. The lavender wool was knitted in st st with the rough side as the right side to emphasise the contrast between the two yarns. The four row bands of lavender were knitted between bands of increasing size of the finer purple yarn. I made a wide band, 12 rows deep, across the back and sleeves to use up the lavender wool.

PATTERN

Size: 34/36 inches (91 cm)
Tension: fine plied yarn, 6 sts to 1 inch (12 sts to 5 cm) no. 9 ($3\frac{3}{4}$ mm) needles. Thick singles, 5 sts to 2 inches (5 sts to 5 cm) no. 0 (8 mm) needles.
Using no. 9 ($3\frac{3}{4}$ mm) needles and fine yarn cast on 196 sts.

97.

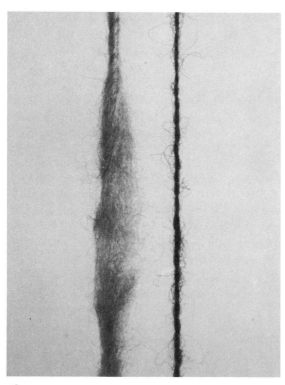

98.

Continue in st st for 1 inch (2.5 cm) ending after a
    P row.
Picot hemline: K 2 tog yf rep from * to * to end.
P 1 row.
Cont in st st until work measures 1 inch (2.5 cm)
    from picot hemline ending after a K row.
Change to thick wool
Cont on no. 9 (3¾ mm) needles but pull up each
    stitch to make large loops. (K 2 tog) twice, K 3
    tog, to end of row (84 sts). Change to no. 0 (8
    mm) needles and work 3 rows st st.
Change to fine yarn and no. 9 (3¾ mm) needles.
* (M1, K1) twice, M2 K1 * (i.e. K into back of next
    st then into front, then into back).
Repeat from * to * to end of row.
Continue in st st for 7 rows.
Change to thick yarn and st st for 4 rows as
    described above.
Work 9 rows in fine yarn.
Work 4 rows in thick yarn.
Work 11 rows in fine yarn.
Work 4 rows in thick yarn.
Work 13 rows in fine yarn.
Work 4 rows in thick yarn.

Work 4 rows in fine yarn.

Right front and sleeve: work in fine yarn on 49 sts casting on 84 sts for sleeve.

Work 10 more rows st st (15 rows altogether)

Work 4 rows st st in thick yarn.

Work 17 rows st st in fine yarn.

Work 1 row thick yarn.

Cast off 3 sts at neck edge on next row.

Dec 1 sts at neck edge on next 2 rows

Work 4 rows in fine yarn dec 1 st at neck edge every row.

Leave stitches on a spare needle.

Work left front to match right, reversing the shapings.

Back: Join fine yarn to middle 98 sts and cast on 84 sts each side for the sleeves.

Continue working bands of thick and fine yarn until back measures same as front.

Cast off middle 30 st st leave remaining sts on needles.

Graft shoulder seams using matching fine yarn.

Using fine yarn and no. 9 needles ($3\frac{3}{4}$ mm) pick up 92 sts evenly up each front and make one inch (2.5 cm) picot hems as at lower edge.

Pick up 72 sts evenly round neck edge and make one inch picot hem.

Sew sleeve seams.

Fold and sl st picot hems to inside.

Make a twisted cord and thread through neck hem. The sleeves may be left as a picot hem, or 2 cords can be made and threaded through the holes in the hem for a gathered cuff.

28 Navajo plied jacket

This jacket has a pink felt yoke and the yarn is Navajo plied to give short, horizontal pink bands across the lower part of the sleeves and jacket.

Navajo plying produces a three-ply yarn from one singles yarn unlike normal plying which gives a two-ply yarn from two singles or a three-ply yarn from three singles. The Navajo method has the advantage of keeping the colours of the plied yarn in the same sequence as that in the singles. Standard plying mixes up the colours and shades, sometimes producing a harsh contrast when a subtle effect would be better. I suppose you could try matching exactly the colours in two singles, but it's not a task I would attempt.

You could, of course, spin a thick singles yarn with the colours in the desired order. But a plied

99.

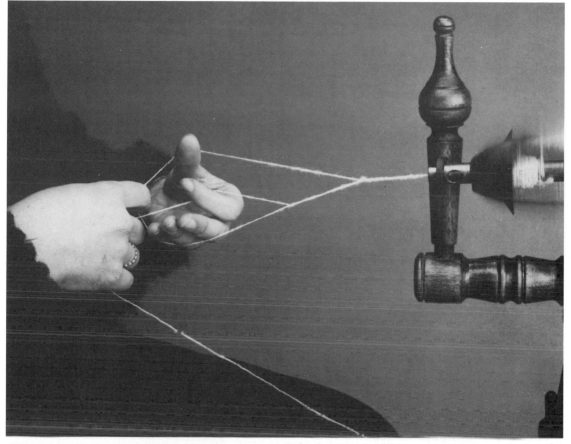

100.

yarn is often preferable for example where extra strength is needed or for use without having to set the twist. Sometimes the fleece lends itself to fine spinning and it is more pleasurable to spin a fine coloured yarn and Navajo ply it than to spin one thick yarn.

Once I had a fleece full of short fibres which clung together in little balls. These were difficult to remove during teasing or carding. I wanted a fairly thick yarn, but found it difficult to spin so thick without including all the short fibres. Small, fuzzy lumps stuck out from the yarn and it looked terrible. The solution was to spin a fine yarn with a long draw. The balls flew off, and those that didn't were easily picked off. This fine yarn was then Navajo plied.

The technique of Navajo plying can be likened to that of making a chain in crocheting, or chaining a long warp. The singles should have slightly more twist in it than a yarn intended for standard plying. Because it is held longer in plying, it loses more twist; as it is handled more, it should not have weak areas. You need the lowest possible wheel ratio to enable your hands to master the technique without the yarn becoming hopelessly overtwisted.

Attach your singles yarn to an empty bobbin on the wheel. Start by making a circle with the yarn, near the orifice. Hold the yarn with your right hand. Bring your left hand up through the circle to catch hold of the yarn with your left index finger (fig. 100). Draw the left hand down, back through the circle, bringing the yarn down and forming a loop. As you do so, hold the bottom

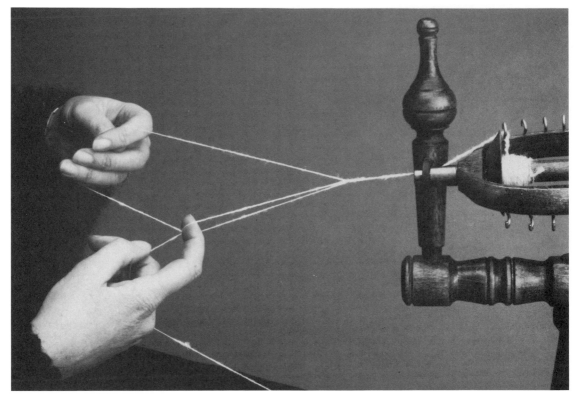

101.

of the circle open with your right hand index finger. Pull the loop down until it is big enough to get your hand through (fig. 101), then let go with your right index finger. Slide your right hand down the yarn until it is level with your left. Now you have completed one 'chain' and are ready to repeat the process by extending your left hand through the newly-formed loop to catch hold of the yarn again, whilst holding open the loop with your right hand, and so on.

Practise making chains without treadling. Then, when you know the sequence of moves, treadle the wheel in the opposite direction to the twist in the singles yarn: if the yarn is Z spun you will be plying with an S twist.

A common mistake when first adding twist is to let the loops get smaller and smaller until you can't get your hand through. So treadle very slowly, with a good draw in tension, and make each loop big enough. After a little practice, you should be able to make a balanced yarn.

For this jacket, I coloured 6 oz (170 g) of a Romney fleece a dusky pink, using a synthetic dye. About $2\frac{1}{2}$oz (55 g) was used to make the felt yoke and the rest was spun with $\frac{3}{4}$ lb (340 g) of brown Suffolk fleece. Several short lengths of pink wool were spun between areas of brown, then a long length of brown was spun before the next group of pink. Each length of pink yarn was spun roughly three times longer than the required pink area in the finally plied yarn. After Navajo plying, the yarn was knitted in stocking stitch. I used the rough side as the right side for my jacket. The pink areas in the yarn formed groups of short lines and made attractive patches of colour which went well with the pink yoke.

Bibliography

SPINNING

Teal, Peter, *Hand Woolcombing and Spinning*, Blandford.

Chadwick, Eileen, *The Craft of Handspinning*, Batsford.

Davenport, Elsie G., *Your Handspinning*, Sylvan Press and Select Books.

Fannin, Allen, *Handspinning Art and Technique*, Van Nostrand Reinhold.

Crocket, Candace, *The Complete Spinning Book*, Watson Guptill.

Jackson, C. and Plowman, J., *The Woolcraft Book*, Collins.

Simmons, Paula, *Spinning and Weaving with Wool*, Pacific Search Press.

Baines, Patricia, *Spinning Wheels, Spinners and Spinning*, Batsford.

Brown, Rachel, *The Weaving, Spinning and Dyeing Book*, Routledge and Kegan Paul.

Hochberg, Bette, *Handspinners Handbook*, Bette and Bernard Hochberg.

Hochberg, Bette, *Fibre Facts*, Bette and Bernard Hochberg.

Hochberg, Bette, *Spin, Span, Spun*, Bette and Bernard Hochberg.

Castino, Ruth A., *Spinning and Dyeing the Natural Way*, Evans Bros.

WEAVING

Collingwood, Peter, *The Techniques of Rug Weaving*, Faber.

Waller, Irene, *Fine Art Weaving*, Batsford.

Tovey, John, *The Technique of Weaving*, Batsford.

Reichard, G. A., *Weaving a Navajo Blanket*, Dover.

Tadek, Beutlich, *The Technique of Woven Tapestry*, Batsford.

Davenport, Elsie G., *Your Handweaving*, Sylvan Press and Select Books.

Sutton, Ann, Collingwood, Peter and St Aubin Hubbard, Geraldine, *The Craft of the Weaver*, BBC Publications.

Simpson and Weir, *The Weaver's Craft*, Dryad Press.

Mattera, Joanne, *Navajo Techniques for Today's Weaver*, Pitman Publishing.

Sutton, Ann and Holtom, Pat, *Tablet Weaving*, Batsford.

Barker, Joan, *Making Plaits and Braids*, Batsford.

Miles, Vera, *Practical Four Shaft Weaving*, Dryad Press

Field, Anne, *Weaving with the Rigid Heddle Loom*, Batsford.

Mattera, Joanne, *Rug Weaving*, Batsford.

Knight, Brian, *Rug Weaving Technique and Design*, Batsford.

DYEING

Dyer, Anne, *Dyes from Natural Sources*, Bell & Hyman.

Wickens, Hetty, *Natural Dyes for Spinners and Weavers*, Batsford.

Robertson, Seonaid, *Dyes from Plants*, Van Nostrand Reinhold.

Wills, Norman, *Woad in the Fens*, Norman Wills.

Lesch, A., *Vegetable Dyeing*, Watson Guptill.

Davenport, Elsie G., *Your Yarn Dyeing*, Sylvan Press and Select Books.

Thurstan, Violetta, *Use of Vegetable Dyes*, Dryad Press

KNITTING AND CROCHET

Norbury, James, *Traditional Knitting Patterns*, Dover.

Stanley, Montse, *Knitting Your Own Designs for a Perfect Fit*, David & Charles.

Don, Sarah, *The Art of Shetland Lace*, Mills & Boon.

Stearns, Ann, *Batsford Book of Crochet*, Batsford.

Shuttleworth, Nina and Biggs, Janet, *Designer Knitting from Handspun Yarns*, Batsford.

OTHERS

Bell, H. S., *Wool*, Pitman.

Ponting, K., *Sheep of the World in Colour*, Blandford.

The National Sheep Association, *British Sheep, British Sheep Breeds, their Wool and its Uses*, British Wool Marketing Board,

Information

Fleeces can be obtained from:

British Wool Marketing Board
Oak Mills, Station Road
Bradford BD14 6JE
West Yorkshire

Your local Guild should be a useful source of information and contacts. For details and addresses write to:

The Association of Guilds of Weavers, Spinners and Dyers
Hon. Sec., Isabella Ricketts
3 Gillsland Road
Edinburgh EH10 5BW
Scotland

The Association's magazine, *The Journal*, also contains advertisements from suppliers of equipment and materials:

The Secretary
The Weavers Journal
Association of Guilds of Weavers, Spinners and Dyers
BCM 963
London WC1N 3XX

Another often useful source is *Crafts* magazine, published by the Crafts Council:

Crafts magazine
8 Waterloo Place
London SW1Y 4AT

Should you still have a problem, write to the author, enclosing a stamped and addressed envelope, c/o the publishers.

HAIR FIBRES

Cottage Crafts
1 Aked Street
Bradford

FLAX AND RAW COTTON

Eliza Leadbeater (address above)

INFORMATION

Animal Breeding Research Organisation
Field Laboratory
Roslin
Midlothian
Scotland

Association of Guilds of Weavers, Spinners and Dyers
c/o Five Bays
10 Stancliffe Avenue
Marford, Wrexham, Clwyd

British Wool Marketing Board
Oak Mills, Station Road
Clayton
Bradford
West Yorkshire

CoSIRA
35 Wimbledon Common
London SW19

Craft Advisory Committee
28 Haymarket
London SW1

Federation of British Craft Societies
British Craft Centre
43 Earlham Street
London WC2

London Guild of Weavers, Spinners and Dyers
c/o 80 Scotts Lane
Bromley
Kent

Index